COMING HOME

the History of Holy Trinity Episcopal Church
Fruitland Park, FL

Ivan Ford

Chetwynd Church Press

Coming Home: the History of Holy Trinity Episcopal Church, Fruitland FL
by Ivan Ford

Published by Chetwynd Church Press
02201 Spring Lake Road
Fruitland Park, FL 34731

www.holytrinityfp.com

First Edition, June 2013

Cover photo by Rod Jones

Author services by Pedernales Publishing, LLC
www.pedernalespublishing.com

ISBN 978-0-61584214-1 Paperback Edition

Printed in the United States of America

Dedication

"Coming Home" is gratefully dedicated to the pioneers here and their relatives abroad who were responsible for the establishment of Holy Trinity and the construction of our building; to the priests and bishops who have served over the years; and to all members, past and present, who have given of their time, talent and other resources to help this church become what it is today.

Contents

Introduction

ALL OF US who attend Holy Trinity have our own stories to tell of how we were drawn to it and why we decided to stay.

There are undoubtedly common denominators in these tales – the beauty, the fellowship, the atmosphere, the feeling that "God is here." (Although God is everywhere, He is often just easier to find in some spots than others.) And, in many instances, the more we become attached to this church, the more we want to know about it. How did such a place come to be?

This book provides the answer to that question. It tells the story of how some young men came to this area to try to get rich, founded Holy Trinity, and ended up enriching not only themselves but many others who came later – including us.

This is the first update of our history since the second edition of Dorothy (Dottie) Paddock's "In the Beauty of Holiness" in 1976.

I had several advantages over Dottie in writing my version. First, I could build on her efforts in many instances by using her excellent book as a source. Secondly, I had a dedicated and skilled researcher and partner in Donna Bott. Anyone who has ever tackled this sort of project knows that research is the biggest and most demanding component of it. Thirdly, Donna and I could tap into resources by using technology that wasn't available in the 1970s. Finally, there is much more history to write about now than there was then.

Some who have been part of Holy Trinity's 125 years are identified by name in the book. However, it would be very hard to cite all the people, and difficult and very time-consuming to interview all current parishioners, who have played a part in making this church what it is today. As far as interviews go, I focused on particular individuals who I thought, collectively, could tell our story. There is no intent to diminish the contributions of anyone else.

Because "Coming Home" is intended more as a recounting of our history than it is as a public relations piece, I included certain happenings that some might like omitted for various reasons. At the same time, I tried to keep my primary audience in mind. On occasion I intentionally excluded a name or left out some details that I believed weren't really necessary to relate.

Everything in this book is told as accurately as (Donna and) I can report it. Because some historical records are missing and others are incomplete, we occasionally had to draw conclusions based on our best knowledge and assessments of situations. But in the process we did our absolute best *not* to follow the adage, "Never let the truth get in the way of a good story." There *are* some good stories in these pages – and, as far as we can determine, these things actually happened.

We initiated this project in early 2010 following Fr. Ted Koelln's arrival at Holy Trinity. I determined soon after the onset that my narrative would end at the time he began his service. Doing so, I felt, would enable me to discuss the interim between Meg Ingalls and him and then leave the happenings of his tenure, in their entirety, for the next update of our history. That way I wouldn't have to sort out ongoing issues and try to put them into context. However, as my work wound down, I began to think it might appear awkward or strange for the tale to conclude in December 2009 and the book not to be published until about three years later. So I decided to write an epilogue – something that I could hold off submitting until the last minute, that would briefly summarize the happenings of 2010 through much of 2012, and that would bring this history more up-to-date.

In addition, right after the epilogue, I have included a short special section called "Lost but Found" that describes a few things that should have appeared in Parts 3 and 4. I discovered, after submitting the text, that I had bypassed these items so I put them in at this location.

As I indicated, Donna and I anticipate that years from now someone else who is as interested in Holy Trinity's history as we are will want to update our work. To that successor we say it's always possible that new pertinent information about what we've covered will come to light later. Furthermore, there's also a chance we have somehow overlooked something of interest or importance. Yet, despite these potential flaws, we trust that our book will be quite helpful to you, just as Dottie's was for us.

All in all we found working on "Coming Home" to be a very rewarding experience and wish our readers the same satisfaction.

Enjoy!

Foreword

I LOVE TO TRAVEL, love to go on trips to places I've never been; or take different roads to places I need to get to once again.

Yet, at the same time, I love coming home. No matter how exciting or fulfilling the trip there is a wonderful sense of relief and comfort in coming home.

Home is the place where I can be me. Not put on some false façade of who I am, not act differently than who I really am.

At the church of the Holy Trinity, there is this strong sense of being one's self. In the last 125 plus years many people have passed through these doors, and many have had this sense of coming home. For some it has been such a relief that it goes beyond mere words to describe. For others, words of homecoming flow freely like the spillway of a dam filled with the spring run-off of an especially snowy winter.

In any case, what a marvelous opportunity we have as we read of the history of this marvelous and special place.

Jesus is here, living among us. People here have chosen to be watchful servants, attentive hearts, loving faces. People here have chosen to open their home of Holy Trinity Church with infinite compassion, with courage to share their faith with those who enter this sacred space, this sacred home..

Here is the church, in its faithfulness, ready to open its doors, to open its members' hearts to all who enter; to all who have come home.

"The Church: historic,
but only because it's old.
Just faith happened here."
Episcopal Haiku

Faith happened/happens here. The word "just" seems out of place to such an incredibly important happening: Faith. We come from many places, many backgrounds and with all that, there is this deep intuition that over and around us stands the Creator, noting our shortcomings, noting our transgressions and yet reassuring us that by His love, and the sharing of that love that we engage in, life, faith is worth sharing!

Join us, come on in, come home – and share your faith, share your love.

Fr. Ted Koelln, Priest-in-charge

Father Ted Koelln

Acknowledgments

A NUMBER of people played roles in bringing this book to fruition.

The following in particular were significant:

Donna Bott did much of the research (as mentioned in the introduction), regularly offered input, made arrangements for production and, in general, coordinated efforts in Florida during the seven months a year the author was absent from the state.

Local historian and writer Rick Reed of Mount Dora gave initial direction to the project and furnished copies of several of his pertinent columns that ran in the Leesburg Daily Commercial.

Lillian Vickers-Smith and Dorothy Paddock wrote earlier histories of Fruitland Park and Holy Trinity, respectively, that are often referenced in these pages.

Various individuals connected with Holy Trinity, past and present, consented to be interviewed for this project and provided valuable content. These persons are listed in the bibliography.

Charlotte Bauer, Dr. Louis Bosanquet, Russell Casson, Betty Hastings, Rod Jones, Dorothy Paddock, Emil Pignetti, Sharon Redding, Richard Sutherland, Carol Wang, the Leesburg Heritage Society, and the Lake County Historical Society contributed pictures for the book. Sue Geiger and Olin Jones of St. James Episcopal Church in Leesburg made some of their archival photos available.

Journalist and editor Susan Ager of Northport, Michigan, thoroughly edited the text using the Associated Press Stylebook. Although not all of her suggestions were incorporated, her input was most beneficial.

Terry Banks, Emil Pignetti, Rod Jones, and Christopher Pelczarski did image enhancements for "Coming Home," and Patti Taylor created the area map.

Rod and Kathy Jones managed the design, formatting and other steps leading to final production, and Bill Stokes helped with the final proofing.

Finally Fr. Ted Koelln (who wrote the foreword) and numerous members of Holy Trinity often asked about the book and were quite encouraging during the roughly two and a half years needed to produce it. Their support made many of the long hours sifting through archives or hunched over a computer seem a little shorter – and definitely more worthwhile.

THANK YOU, everyone!

Part 1: 1875-1895

Early Fruitland Park

IN 1875, with the Civil War having been over for ten years, Recon-struction in the South was nearing conclusion. However, that was hardly a concern for Maj. Orlando P. Rooks. The horticulturist had other interests in the region as he and his wife, Josephine, attended a lecture in Cincinnati. The two were thinking of leaving Ohio to improve his health. The presentation they heard was a promotion sponsored by the legislature of Florida. Speaker Capt. J.C. Kendricks touted one place in particular, a spot called Eldorado (located off present-day Highway 441 on Lake Harris, a little southwest of the Leesburg Airport.) Rooks and his wife, enthralled by the description, arrived in Florida in January 1876 eager to buy. With a party of tourists under Kendricks' direction, they went by boat and then hack to Leesburg. They were reportedly so impressed by the countryside that they decided to homestead just north of town and forgo Eldorado.

Rooks was responsible for calling their new settlement Fruitland Park, and the main roadway Berckman Street. The names came from the Fruitland Nurseries of Augusta, Ga., and its owner, J.P. Berckman, a friend of Rooks.

Postal authorities had a problem shortly thereafter. They refused to recognize the hamlet's name since there was already a Fruitland in Florida near Palatka. Consequently, the name was changed to Gardenia in 1884.

Unfortunately, a railroad built through the little community just prior to the change had listed the place as Fruitland Park in all its printed matter and refused to recognize the *new* name. As a result, all rail shipments had to be addressed to Fruitland Park and all regular mail to Gardenia. This situation created much confusion until 1888 when a petition to postal authorities to change the name back to Fruitland Park was granted.

Rooks, his brother William A. and Granville Stapylton were pivotal in the establishment of a railroad in this area. In 1883, they persuaded the Florida Southern Railroad Co. to run a line through town instead of on the other side of Dead River (now the boundary between Leesburg and Tavares) as originally planned.

The desire for rail service was twofold. First, the men were hoping to make significant money growing citrus and needed a way to get the crop to Ocala where it could be shipped to market. Reportedly three-quarters of the Florida citrus crop was shipped from that town. And, secondly, they wanted a means to attract more potential residents and investors to this area.

Until about the late 1850s cotton and sugar cane had been the predominant agricultural products in the region. But, sometime about then, growers began turning citrus production into a very profitable venture in a number of locales in northern and particularly central Florida.

One of these locations was Fruitland Park. Although there had been a few groves nearby before 1876, more began appearing about the time of Rooks' arrival, with greater growth in the 1880s. Stapylton was among the men most responsible for the boom.

A young "Founding Father"

One often imagines a "Founding Father" as an older, august, learned individual. Granville Brian Chetwynd-Stapylton might qualify on the second count and definitely would on the third. But the ambitious entrepreneur was only 22 years old when he came to central Florida in 1881. Everything indicates that he arrived fully expecting to make a considerable amount of money. He did that by not only participating directly in the "citrus rush" but also by buying and selling real estate, and by developing an English Colony, one of a number of such groups stretching across Central Florida at the time. For instance, there were three other such colonies just in what is now Osceola County.

Granville Brian Chetwynd-Stapylton

Stapylton was born Dec. 11, 1858, in Malden, Surrey, near London, where his father, the Rev. William Chetwynd-Stapylton, served as the vicar of Old Malden Parish and St. John the Baptist Church, Worcester Park. Granville was an honor student at Haileybury College.

One of his projects in Florida was a subdivision which was surveyed on July 1, 1884, and platted into 39 lots of various sizes surrounding Lake Ella (probably named for his sister), located about two miles north of Holy Trinity Church. The first lot was sold in late 1885 to the Rev. William R. Cosens, father of Francis Cosens, a founder of Holy Trinity.

Stapylton had also purchased 80 acres for $2,200 from John Henderson Tanner, a freed slave and one of four brothers (also including Samuel, Martin and Henry) who lived in an area called Tannersville in the immediate vicinity of Holy Trinity. The brothers had originally homesteaded 160 acres each.

The property acquired from Henderson Tanner was around what was then

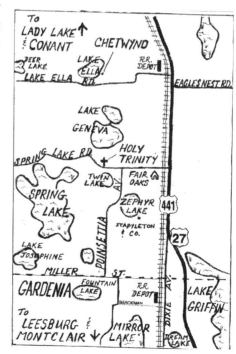

Map showing English settlement (drawn by Patti Taylor)

called Skillet Pond, soon renamed Zephyr Lake. This location is southeast of the church on the east side of the present Poinsettia Road. In conjunction with partners Cyril Francis Herford, 19, and Hugh Sandeman Budd, 28, and under the name of Stapylton and Co., Stapylton built a large boarding house, a dining hall with an attached kitchen, and stables. This facility was for young English bachelors who came to the area to study the art and craft of citrus growing. These students paid $30 rent and $30 tuition each month, a goodly amount for that period.

Stapylton and Budd were among the founders of Holy Trinity.

Famed Florida author Marjorie Kinnan Rawlings later referred to the settlers as "remittance men" in her book "Golden Apples." This reference reportedly didn't sit well. Remittance men were considered to be young Englishmen, basically "black sheep", who received a stipend as long as they stayed out of their native country.

Stapylton and Co., c1887

Left to right: Stable, boarding house, and dining hall with an attached kitchen

According to Alfred Bosanquet, a member of a key family of Holy Trinity, "The young men who came here were interested in grove culture, travel and a new country, and were sons of good English families."

The connotation of this term has now changed from the intent that Rawlings allegedly had.

Along with his business interests, Stapylton had other intentions at the time. He was attracted to Elizabeth Routledge, five years his senior, who lived across Zephyr Lake with her sister and married brother and family. Following courtship, the two were married on Dec.15, 1885, at Elizabeth's brother James' home. A Methodist clergyman, C.I.R. Vandewater of Gardenia, officiated. The only others present were Elizabeth's local family and Stapylton's partners, Herford and Budd.

Elizabeth (known as Lizzie) later wrote to her sister Emily (whom she called Embly) in England: "It was a wedding after my own heart – unconventional to a degree and therefore all the more enjoyable. You asked me what I wore. When anyone asked me what I was going to be married in, I told them 'dark blue.' So I was – *in riding habit.* Granville and his partners wore their riding clothes also. As soon as it was over we joined a huge riding party of about 58 people, nearly the whole of our English colony . . . We started from Granville's old house . . . We rode through the woods to Conant, about 6 miles off, where we had an informal luncheon. I shall never forget the bright picture it made, looking back at any turn in the road to see the whole cavalcade streaming through the trees, the horses of all colours, their riders most of them fine-looking men with their white riding breeches shining in the sun, and the woods perfectly gorgeous with the autumn tints of every conceivable shade of red and gold and brown and grey and green."

The luncheon served as their wedding reception. She also mentioned in her letter, in further emphasizing their "being unconventional," that they did not take a honeymoon.

Later in the same correspondence, in describing her husband, she wrote: "Above middle height, straight and square, fair hair, blue eyes, small fair mustache, a handsome face with a grave expression and altogether of an aristocratic appearance, and no wonder, for his family traces their descent from before the Conquest. He is rather quiet to outsiders but I don't find him so. I think we are something alike in some things; for instance most people think us both very reserved excepting those who know us best."

The couple had two children—a son, Granville Brian (called by his middle name), in 1887 and a daughter, Ella Mabel, in 1889.

Stapylton ventured into the financial world in April 1886 when the firm of Morrison, Stapylton & Co. opened a private or convenience bank in a general store in Leesburg, at that time a town of about 900 people. With original partner Cyril Herford having moved to another English Colony in middle Tennessee a few months prior, Stapylton joined in this undertaking with Hugh Sandeman Budd and William Hiram Morrison, a New York real estate attorney who spent his winters in Florida. Following Morrison's retirement, this bank was incorporated as the Leesburg and County State Bank in 1890 with Stapylton as president, Budd as cashier and Robert Francis Edward (Frank) Cooke, also a founder of Holy Trinity, as assistant cashier.

In 1895 Stapylton moved to Leesburg. He and his family lived in the St. James Episcopal Church rectory for a time after it was first built. This change in residency may have been prompted by a struggle to keep the bank solvent, not only because of an economic depression going on at the time but also due to closely-occurring freezes in late 1894 and early 1895 that completely devastated citrus production, ending it for over ten years. Every other bank within 50 miles of Leesburg closed, but not Stapylton's. Although deposits dropped from $175,000 to below $40,000 in four years, he kept the doors open.

Maintained William T. Kennedy in his 1929 book, "The History of Lake County, Florida," "Everlasting credit is due to the able management of the bank officials in practically saving the city of Leesburg from financial ruin at this time."

Two banks in Ocala were among those suffering huge calamities in the mid-1890s. The assets of both institutions were assigned to Stapylton as a receiver.

A featured speaker at the Florida Bankers' Convention in 1896, he said: "It is difficult to exaggerate the moral and material injury that a community sustains by a bank failure. The worst side of human nature is unfailingly brought out and exhibits itself naked and unashamed. Loss of faith in mankind and in the stability of all human institutions follows a bank failure and renders many of its victims, for a time at least, cynical, suspicious, and unreasonable. The shock to public confidence does incalculable harm to the cause of banking."

A paragraph in a 1926 Leesburg Commercial story about local

banks says of Stapylton, "He had the characteristics that in those days were popularly attributed to bankers, being aloof and formal in business hours, but he was staunch in his friendships and the soul of his honor."

By 1900 Stapylton had become involved in the establishment of an Ocala Colony in Cuba. Sometime early in January of that year, he and his wife moved to Havana for business reasons; the children had returned to England for school. While there, both Stapyltons contracted yellow fever. Still they came back to Leesburg in April, 1901. By early the following year he was chosen as the town's mayor. But his health remained poor and, in July 1902, according to The Ocala Evening Star, he and his family left for England to visit friends on the "other side of the water and to recruit his failing health."

The Leesburg and County State Bank received a cable Oct. 31, 1902, announcing the death of its president by tuberculosis at his father's home two days prior. Stapylton was 44.

His estate was appraised at $2,139.55. It was bequeathed in its entirety to his wife.

Elizabeth and their two children remained in England where she died June 29, 1943. Brian passed away in 1964 and Ella in 1974.

What and where was Chetwynd?

Chetwynd was a location in the late 1800s that included Gardenia/Fruitland Park and was closely entwined with the establishment of Holy Trinity. But what exactly, and where precisely, was it?

Read various articles and books and the writers don't seem to agree, other than that it was named for Granville Chetwynd-Stapylton. Several different interpretations have been passed off as fact: It has been called a town, a subdivision and the name of the whole English Colony in this immediate vicinity.

In essence it was all three.

As reported previously, Stapylton and his partners had erected a boarding house and related facilities on Zephyr Lake for the young English bachelors who comprised the bulk of the 80 or so people who came and went from this area before the end of the 1880s. As a whole, this group was referred to locally as the English Colony.

In addition, Stapylton decided to develop a subdivision on Lake Ella, about two miles north of Holy Trinity, and this project was called Chetwynd. As platted, the development completely surrounded the lake.

The Chetwynd Arms Hotel, open for a season.

He is also said to have been instrumental in the establishment of the post office of Chetwynd on June 9, 1887. This office was the first in Lake County; Lake had been formed from Sumter and Orange counties and set off just two months earlier.

According to William Kennedy in "The History of Lake County, Florida," there were seven or eight stores in the vale of Chetwynd Hill, plus the Chetwynd Arms Hotel on the Lake Ella waterfront.

In addition, a general store was located near the railroad station. This store and the depot were to the east of Stapylton's subdivision and the other commercial establishments.

The Chetwynd Depot near present-day US Route 441/27.

In an early letter to his father, Frank Cooke noted that that these businesses collectively, along with the subdivision, constituted a village. "They are building a new town of Chetwynd," said Cooke, who would later go on to become a prominent banker in Leesburg.

Although both Fruitland Park and later Lady Lake would eventually "claim" it, the townsite of Chetwynd today is located within the latter municipality's city limits.

Holy Trinity's records indicate that, within a few years of the subdivision's establishment, the name Chetwynd was often used to refer to the entire colony. As an example, part of a letter of church business written in September 1888 by Thomas A. Vincent, secretary-treasurer of the vestry, says, "The want of an Episcopal church and clergyman in the English Colony now known as the Colony of Chetwynd, Lake Co., Fla . . ."

To further complicate matters, there were two other development operations in the vicinity of Stapylton's subdivision by the mid-to-late 1880s: the Chetwynd Land Co. and the Chetwynd Improvement Co. While Stapylton may have been a major player in some respects in one or both of these businesses, there is no evidence he had a legal interest in either.

The Chetwynd Land Co. intended to develop a subdivision directly west of Lake Ella, but records show this venture never got off the ground. The Chetwynd Improvement Co. planned to build a town called Dundee immediately to the east and contiguous to the Stapylton subdivision. Dundee was to extend across what is now US 27/441 and then north toward Lady Lake. It also never really materialized.

In addition, there was another little community nearby—Conant—which was composed mostly of Americans who had migrated there from northern states but did have some upper-crust British residents.

Established in 1884 by the Sumter County Florida Land Co., it stretched from Lady Lake to the Marion County line. Conant was the location of Granville and Elizabeth Stapylton's wedding luncheon. The settlement boasted a luxurious three-story hotel catering to the area's upper class who, it was said, made a practice of snobbery, looking down in particular on orange growers.

Stapylton maintained a connection with this community from its inception. In early 1882, the U.S. Government granted 320 acres of land to him in what was to become Conant.

As was mentioned previously, Stapylton had helped persuade the Florida Southern Railroad Co. to construct a line in this area. Two years after his receipt of the government grant, he sold some of that acreage to the railroad who proceeded to build tracks running right through the middle of Conant, essentially paralleling both US 27/441 and County Road 25. Then, with Stapylton donating some land from his Chetwynd compound, the line continued on through one side of Chetwynd Colony to Fruitland Park. The month after the first sale, the entrepreneur sold the remainder of his grant land to the Sumter County Florida Land Co., of which he was corresponding secretary.

Most of Conant's territory that is not in present-day Lady Lake is a small part of The Villages.

Life in the Colony

People undertake life on a frontier for a variety of reasons. Sometimes the purpose is to make money, and that was certainly the case in this area's English Colony in the late 1800s. But such a life is often tedious and filled with long hours of hard work; it is not nearly as romantic as some accounts would have readers believe.

An early member of Holy Trinity, Lillian Vickers-Smith, who was employed by the Leesburg Commercial, authored "The History of Fruitland Park" in 1924. In describing the young Englishmen, she said, "They were a happy, care-free group upon whose shoulders responsibility rested very lightly."

But actual correspondence from two of the Colony members sheds a different light on the matter.

George Winter wrote his mother shortly after arrival about living in this area, and Frank Cooke penned several letters to his father on the same subject. Cooke, as was mentioned previously, eventually went on to become a noted Leesburg banker while Winter, seemingly more of a sportsman than a scholar, was sent to Florida after his aunt paid a premium to Stapylton to take him as a pupil.

One can imagine that the young men who left the comfort of their families and homes in England to settle here and grow citrus had probably never encountered such conditions as met them upon arrival. They were exposed to excessive heat, torrential rains, swarms of mosquitoes and other bugs, and wild animals that roamed the land and ate their crops.

On one occasion Cooke wrote, "This is a nether region. Because of it we have not been obliged to adapt civilized manners such as wearing coats and ties at dinner."

Both men arrived in 1886, Winter getting here a month before Cooke, and both initially roomed at Stapylton's boarding house on Zephyr Lake. Cooke had land to clear and crops to plant. Winter, on the other hand, soon bought a "barren piece of land surrounded by pines." He built a house on it and at first started cultivating oranges.

Cooke, in talking about owning land and raising citrus, said, "I shall be able to get one (parcel) of a very large size but the clearing and planting and then *waiting* take such a fearfully long time that only the Methuselah of the place can hope to make much out of it and no doubt their grandchildren will help them." Later, in discussing the same topic, he added, "If possible I shall try to find a place that has been started. At any rate the older the better."

George Dawson, Alfred Stanley, George Back and Mesey Fellows work a grove at Stapylton & Company, c1887..

Winter wrote, "I don't think I would ever do anything at orange growing as it wants some capital to start, something like £100 (equivalent to $487) a year for ten years, then a grove would begin paying, it is like most things, it wants some capital and a lot of energy and the one I haven't got and the other is very scarce. I am learning the blacksmith's trade which I hope will come in useful to me somewhere."

Winter developed into a rather colorful character. He grew ferns and pines for the New York market and was referred to as "the wild man of the woods," having a small steamboat that he used for fishing. In addition, he had a photograph of a large crocodile which he had killed and stuffed, strapping it to a sizable basket-chair with a big straw hat on its head and a churchwarden's pipe in its mouth. He was most acclaimed, though, for one of his trees that withstood a severe frost that killed all the other trees for miles around and was still alive and bearing in the 1950s.

Some years after the "Colony period" he was among the various local residents who hunted with Annie Oakley and her husband during the famous sharpshooter's visits to Leesburg.

Cooke, meanwhile, wanted to buy out an existing photo business in Leesburg to provide income until "our groves begin to pay." He intended "to be able to make my camera pay all my current expenses and to do that I must set up in some town or travel around the country, for I can see that this colony is at present too poor to go in for many luxuries." His father was against Cooke's venture into the photo business because "it's too risky to put so much money in such a speculation." Cooke replied, "Well, everything out here is a speculation." Fortunately for history, he pursued his plan, eventually setting up his own dark room. He is probably responsible for most of the photographs taken in this area during this period.

Both Cooke and Winter wrote of long days, of rising before 5 a.m. and working until 8 or 10 p.m., saying, "I have been so awfully busy . . . that I have scarcely a moment to spare" and "You can imagine how tired I am now."

Cooke's responsibilities included raising cows and chickens. Initially he was optimistic about the profits to be made from these animals. "We have a large number of poultry, and eggs are always in demand," he explained. "And I think we shall sell all the milk we want." His expectations were partly based on an anticipated market in close proximity. He noted the new town of Chetwynd being built nearby and how they hoped to supply it.

But, in less than a year, his enthusiasm was souring.

"Fowls don't pay out here," he claimed. "We started with 300 (chickens) and now have 4 doz. Which I think is at least 36 too many. Would almost give them away to get rid of them."

As far as the cows were concerned, he said, "What (they) are going to do I don't know . . . We sell only about 9 quarts a day at present at an average of 12 ½ cents a quart."

At one point he apparently tried to get rid of most of his herd. "If I can't sell the cows I'll turn them out into the woods," he remarked. This was a common practice at the time.

Cooke also commented on health conditions in the area. In one instance he said he thought everyone was in quarantine because of yellow fever and another time mentioned the threat of cholera. Later, in discussing the quality of medical care, he claimed that "doctors out here are promoted vets."

Concerning the weather, Cooke wrote, "The rain has at last descended and we are thankful, but woe unto the man who is caught out in one of the showers minus a waterproof." On another occasion he noted that the temperature was 100 degrees in the shade. And about the bugs he remarked, "The house is now so hermetically sealed against insects that we can sit in comfort on the porch. We have been living for the past two weeks on corn and cabbage salad."

He described the "horrid" after-effects of the significant freeze in 1889. It's ironic that about a year earlier he had written, "It seems so funny reading about the frost and snows that you are having when we are getting green peas and strawberries."

There apparently was a kind of cowboy mentality in this area— at least a bit like what existed in the American West at the same time.

Cooke noted, "We went down to Brooksville during the 'convention' which consists of the delegates from all the different counties meeting to select a member for Congress. Happily, it passed off very quietly, as pistols were only drawn twice during the proceedings."

Stapylton encountered a similar situation at a later convention in Leesburg when he supported the opposing side of a political argument. A man drew a gun and threatened to shoot but was quickly disarmed.

On the lighter side, the colonists received mail from home at least twice a week. And despite their hard work and long hours, they had occasional free time. Social outlets were developed to fill their need for recreation.

One of the first was the Forest Club which was started in 1883 and met in a structure erected on Spring Lake. The clubhouse was well equipped, having a reading room and a billiard table among other things. But this group disbanded within a few years, reportedly because of high dues and restrictive qualifications for membership. Then the Bucket and Dipper Club was established on June 2, 1885;

it lasted into 1901. Eventually it began meeting in the Forest Club's building, then decided to buy the facility. After the purchase, the new owners added a tennis court.

The Bucket and Dipper Club was also limited for a period of time to British-born men or their sons, and they had to be approved for admission. At some point, according to Lillian Vickers-Smith in her "History of Fruitland Park," "The qualifications for membership were not observed so strictly." In addition, the organization didn't have the high dues charged by the Forest Club. Most likely one reason for the lower fees was the limited refreshments offered at meetings. The only thing usually available was a bucket of cold water and a tin dipper. However, one section of the group's by-laws states, "It shall be the power of the Committee by special leave or cause shown, to authorize moderate refreshment on any occasions." It is known that lemonade was served in some instances but there is no record of anything more.

There were 19 charter members including Stapylton and various other founders and early members of Holy Trinity. Attendance at general meetings averaged about 40.

The club held meetings, dances, parties, debates, concerts and "theatricals." Games were also played with chess and whist being among the favorites. There was a strict "no gambling" rule.

About one of the dances Cooke remarked, "They were talking about (it) but have concluded they can't get it up before Lent. So it is to be postponed until Easter. It's a great nuisance that Lent should come just at the best time of year."

Debates were very popular and covered a variety of subjects. Among these were "Abolition of the House of Lords," "Mormonism," "The Decadence of the British Empire," "Compulsory Military Service," "Naturalization" and "Women's Suffrage." (Stapylton supported suffrage but the group as a whole eventually passed a motion stating that suffrage was "inexpedient and the application of it mischievous.")

Over the years attendance waned periodically at the activities and at the several meetings held annually. There were a myriad of reasons for this, including members being in England, commitments to church-related meetings, competition from the Forest Club and conflicts with other social activities.

When the vote came up in 1891 on whether to purchase the Forest Club's building, Stapylton spoke against the proposal, citing the quality of "entertainments" currently being provided by the organization. The group's leaders repudiated his accusations and were roundly supported by the rest of the membership. Perhaps those in charge concurred with Cooke's earlier assessment that people were not very critical of the concerts: "They relieve the monotony of things in general." Thereafter Stapylton attended no more meetings.

Although the Forest Club and the Bucket and Dipper Club were more prominent, the Colony also had a painting club, something called the "Moonlight Series," and a drama club known as "The Chetwynd Strollers." Nothing further is available about these entities.

After Holy Trinity was established, church-going gradually took on some social overtones. Cooke commented in July 1890, "Most of the Colony are now happy and today (being Sunday) have been swaggering to church in their latest London fashions."

Hunting and horse racing were other favorite pursuits of the settlers. The earliest racing activity may have occurred on a track just west of Stapylton's subdivision on Lake Ella. Not long thereafter, though, the young Englishmen, together with some businessmen in Leesburg, formed the ABC (American, British and Colonial) Racing Association. Races were held beginning in 1888, first on a track just outside Montclair and thereafter also on one on Picciola Island. Montclair was a town with a reported population of 2,000 in 1889 (although that figure seems high in light of other information known today). It was located west of Leesburg on what is now County Road 468 (south of Griffin Road and north of 44/West Main Street). The Picciola Island facility was established on property that is presently a part of the Methodist Church's Life Enrichment Center.

The picture below shows a type of racing that involves hurdling obstacles and is known today as steeplechase. But the association also held some unusual events like Cheroot Stakes, Egg and Spoon and even a mule race.

A Sunday bareback hurdle race at Picciola Island c1887.
Left to right: Reginald Strachey, S.H.A. Willis(winner), William Trimble,
Alfred Stanley, George Elin.

The "buggy enclosure" at Montclair, Feb. 9,1888.

Sundays seemed to be preferred days for racing. And this, in part, may have led up to the founding of Holy Trinity, claimed Alfred Bosanquet.

In an article by current Lake County historian Rick Reed that appeared in the Leesburg Daily Commercial, Bosanquet is quoted as saying, "According to a story that I heard often as a child, to these races go some of the credit for building Holy Trinity Church. It seems that a visiting clergyman from England came to the colonies to see how the sons of his friends were doing in a new country . . . He found most of the young Englishmen out racing their horses on Sunday afternoon" (which would have been the time of many of the services then).

The founding of Holy Trinity

Whether horse racing was in part responsible for the founding of Holy Trinity is conjecture. It does make for a good story but research does not conclusively prove that theory. What is known is that, after the appearance of the first Englishmen in 1881, opportunities for Anglican/Episcopal worship were virtually non-existent until the arrival from Orlando at least four years later of the Rev. John Baptiste Caillerrier Beaubien. Beaubien initially served St. Thomas in Eustis, the newly formed St. James Church in Leesburg, Grace Chapel in Gardenia, and churches in Brooksville, Yalaha, and Astatula.

A 1951 brief history of Holy Trinity, also written by Lillian Vickers-Smith, states that in the mid-1880s, a clergyman from England came to see how the young men of the colony were getting along. This individual could have been any of several persons—possibly Spencer Fellows who baptized the Stapyltons' son, or perhaps Stapylton's father who visited in September 1885. At any rate, at about that time, a meeting was called for the purpose of organizing a church. This gathering was held in June or July 1886, depending on which record is correct, at Stapylton's dining hall on Zephyr Lake.

According to the original vestry minute book, written by Thomas A. Vincent, secretary and treasurer, "The want of an Episcopal Church and clergyman in the English Colony, known as the Colony of Chetwynd . . . had been for some time felt, and a movement had been made to obtain subscriptions to erect a church in the colony. The only available services were some few held by the Rev. Dr. Beaubien at Leesburg and Gardenia, and these being considered as of too irregular a type to fit our needs, a general meeting of the colony was called . . . to discuss what steps should be taken to provide the neighborhood with a church and rector."

A subsequent general meeting occurred in August 1886 at the same place. At this session Stapylton, at the request of those attending, agreed to contact the Rev. John Campbell Wheatley Tasker of Somerset, Kent, England, as a future chaplain. Tasker had been recommended to the group. The first conversation about the building site took place then; this allegedly turned into a somewhat contentious discussion that lasted several months.

Fund-raising for the proposed church, which had not yet been named, began almost immediately. A letter dated Aug. 22, 1886, and signed by a five-member building committee, was sent to family members, relatives and friends in England to solicit subscriptions, and this request was "responded to most generously." Then on Sept. 7 of that year, at a general meeting of the Bucket and Dipper Club, a proposal by Kenneth Streatfield, a member of the building committee, carried unanimously and provided that "admission be charged for entertainments for the purpose of raising a fund towards buying an organ for the church."

A concert was held April 18, 1887, to bring in money and that was followed shortly by a bazaar in early July on the vicarage grounds of Stapylton's father's church in Old Malden. This latter event provided most of the capital to build Holy Trinity. However, it has been said that the young horsemen of Chetwynd may have contributed part of their racetrack winnings as well.

As the fund-raising continued, Tasker arrived from England. In December 1886 he met and consulted twice with the Bishop of Florida, Edwin Gardner Weed, and with the bishop's consent held the first services for Holy Trinity Mission.

The first service was one of Evening Prayer. It took place at Stapylton's dining hall at 3 p.m. on Dec. 19, 1886, with 50 in attendance.

The second occurred Jan. 2, 1887, at the Forest Club's clubhouse. There were again 50 in the congregation with 19 communicants.

Note that only baptized and confirmed Anglicans could receive Holy Communion.

Services alternated between these two locations until Sunday, Jan. 23, 1887, when a temporary church was established in John Vickers-Smith's barn on Lake Geneva. The first services there attracted 39 people for Morning Prayer and Communion at 11 a.m. (a Morning Prayer/Communion combination was common then and for quite a while thereafter) and 15 for Evening Prayer and a Litany at 3:30 p.m.

John Vickers-Smith's barn on Lake Geneva, 1887.

The barn's altar hangings are now preserved in shadowboxes in the church.

Since the settlers regularly rode their horses to church, they started a tradition of standing during the offertory. This practice, which lasted until 1945, allowed the wearers of snug-fitting riding breeches to more easily retrieve their offertory money from their pockets.

Late in January, the site for the permanent church was selected with land transactions recorded March 24, 1887. Located about halfway between the two groups to be served – the residents of the Lake Ella and Fruitland Park areas – it was an acre of land, later called the church acre, which was purchased for $20 from land homesteaded by freed slave Samuel Tanner and his wife, Alice.

The Tanners also sold for $550, in March, 14.36 acres contiguous to the church acre to Tasker's daughter in trust for her father throughout his natural life. In 1894 Elizabeth Tasker and her brother Duncan sold this land to William Crane Gray, missionary bishop of Southern Florida, for $5. With policy dictating that the diocese owns such land in trust for a member church, this meant that the diocese allowed Holy Trinity to have the additional acreage.

Sometime early in 1887, following the site selection, a three-person vestry was named with Granville Chetwynd-Stapylton as senior warden, Alexander Cazalet as junior warden and Thomas A. Vincent as secretary/treasurer. In those days the bishop appointed the vestry members upon recommendation rather than having the congregation elect them; this practice continued until Holy Trinity became a parish in the 1960s.

It was also apparently common at that time for a clergyman to receive offertories at services in lieu of, or a supplement to, a stipend. On Ash Wednesday 1887, Tasker noted that he was to get the offertories, which averaged about $5, each Sunday.

The first baptisms in the mission, which was still meeting in the barn, occurred on Easter Sunday, April 10, 1887, "according with the rites of the Episcopal Church of England and America." Three daughters of James and Elizabeth Routledge, formerly of London, were baptized. These girls were the nieces of Elizabeth Stapylton. Dorothy had been born June 20, 1883; Audrey Sept. 14, 1884; and Brenda Nov. 22, 1885.

At a general meeting held in September 1887, the congregation voted for a sum of $1,500 for building and approved $1,000 for investment for the clergyman's salary.

In a letter to his father a few months earlier, Frank Cooke had expressed displeasure about the solicitation of funds for the latter purpose. "I was very much annoyed at your receiving a begging letter about the parson's stipend, and which I find has been sent to everyone's people without our knowledge. I think you have done quite enough for the church and I think we ought to be able to keep this old parson."

Vestry secretary/treasurer Vincent later noted, "In consequence of incoming subscriptions we have been able to increase the amount devoted to building to $2,150 at which figure the contract for the present church has been given out to Mr. E. Thompson of Savannah, Georgia, the nominee of Mr. John J. Nevitt, architect of the same place & designer of the accepted plans . . . The church is now in course of construction of the management of the above-named builder." Subsequent vestry minutes state that Holy Trinity was erected during the spring and summer of 1888.

The entire building inside and out is made of yellow pine in a Gothic design often called "Florida" or "Carpenter" Gothic, a modification of an English style adapted to the materials and conditions of the period and area.

The exterior is characterized by fish scale shingles, pointed-arch windows and steep gables. It has always been painted white but has had various colors of trim throughout the years.

The interior wood was much lighter in the early days but has darkened appreciably over time.

Other interesting architectural features include three nearly identical porches and a since-removed bell tower.

The total cost of the church ended up being about $2,500.

Holy Trinity Episcopal Mission, Chetwynd, Fla., c1889.

It has been suggested that the porches to the north and the south help dissipate the sideward thrust of the walls. The doors to these porches point more-or-less toward Lake Ella and Fruitland Park, locations of the two groups of people the church hoped to serve. In the past the south door was the primary entry while the west one was used only for special occasions. Following the paving of Spring Lake Road and the construction of the road to the rectory, the west door became the primary entrance in 1961.

Although the church had a tower, the tower did not contain a bell. This belfry was removed in the 1920s following countless problems with bats, lightning strikes and roof leaks.

A railroad bell of no particular historical significance is currently in use in front of the church. No one seems to know much about this bell or when it was acquired. It may, however, have been the bell donated by the Atlantic Coast Line Railroad in 1953 to St. James Church "for use in its mission stations."

The first boy to be baptized—on Oct. 30, 1887—was the Stapyltons' son Granville Brian who had been born about six weeks earlier. Presiding was Spencer Fellows, a clergyman from Norfolk, England, who had purchased land in Stapylton's subdivision. He arrived shortly before this service.

The church's parish register records the first burial as taking place on Dec. 3, 1887. James Smith, 74, formerly of London, was interred in the church acre with the Rev. C.I.R. Vandewater officiating. Vandewater had preached the first Methodist sermon under a tree in Fruitland Park and then helped found the local Methodist Church. This church, according to Lillian Vickers-Smith's history, was the oldest in Fruitland Park/Gardenia. Now called Community Methodist Church, it is in a different location. Holy Trinity embraced ecumenism even then; Vandewater was nearby and much easier to reach than Fr. Beaubien.

In January 1888 Holy Trinity started a men's choir, and a weekly celebration of Holy Communion began.

Later that year, the vestry deemed Bishop Weed's response regarding the appointment of a clergyman to be vague. Stapylton, as senior warden, was directed to write the bishop a letter asking if "we may take steps to supply our parish with a minister and to decide parish limits." (In England a parish was a defined area with the church at its center.) On Oct. 31, 1888, the vestry determined that the bishop had ignored the senior warden's appeal and decided on its own to place a priest-wanted advertisement in English church newspapers. The ad appeared in December.

At 3 p.m. on Dec. 2, 1888, the first Sunday of Advent, Holy Trinity Mission of Chetwynd held its initial service in its newly-constructed building. Joseph Julian, who by then had become the first resident priest at St. James in Leesburg, led "ordinary Evensong." The congregation of 40 gave an offering totaling $4.96.

The interior of the mission church, c1889. Note the organ on the left and the choir pews.

How the church came to be called Holy Trinity is not known. Usually the mission picks the church name. It can be speculated that, in this case, "Holy Trinity" was chosen because this was the major feast day closest to the founding.

Improvements to the church building and grounds were apparently ongoing as they seem to be to this day. Vestry secretary Vincent wrote that on Dec. 22, 1888, "... determined to fence church acre setting the south fence 30 feet back from boundary line and setting a double gate in the centre of the south fence; put hitching posts on south fence; seat the church half way back down the nave and put in stalls and reading desk; buy kneeler for communicants and make inquiries about altar rails; to have leaks in bell turret repaired; obtain lamps for the choir and furnish the vestry room for the minister; to oil the floor and erect a shed for harnesses, saddles, etc." A notation for March 10, 1889, indicates that "stabling" was to be built in the northeast corner of the church yard.

There was a new organ in February 1889. For Easter Sunday that year, according to the secretary, "the church was prettily decorated and the new seats were used for the first time. A congregation of 75 was present."

Holy Trinity was consecrated by Bishop Weed on Friday, July 12, 1889. Vincent wrote, "The church was tastefully decorated and the service as choral as our singing capacity admitted of. The weather tho very hot was beautifully fine. The Bishop afterwards held a reception at Messrs. Stapylton and Budd's hall." There were 26 communicants and an offering of $10.34.

The first rector

Although the image of the circuit-riding preacher may be more closely associated with the Methodist church, Episcopalians in this vicinity certainly had firsthand experience.

Regardless of whether they were called circuit riders, Fr. Beaubien and Joseph Ernest Julian actually were such individuals. As indicated in the previous section, Beaubien served at other locations besides Leesburg and Gardenia. Julian, who became the first rector of Holy Trinity, did likewise. (Apparently the title "vicar," which is what he actually was here, wasn't in use at that time.)

Born Josef Schullian in 1840 in Prussia, Julian graduated from the University of Virginia and Gambier (Ohio) Seminary and was initially called from a parish in Marion, Ohio, to be the priest of St. James in Leesburg. St. James was organized about half a year earlier than was Holy Trinity, but its building wasn't completed until in 1889 and wasn't consecrated until May 2, 1897. Although Julian would remain based in Leesburg, in short order, and probably for logistical/financial reasons, his responsibilities expanded to include Holy Trinity, St. John the Baptist in Montclair, St. Stephen's in Yalaha, Union Chapel at Corley Island and St. John's in Brooksville.

The Rev. Joseph Ernest Julian, c1872

St. James and Holy Trinity were yoked for the first time under Beaubien. This arrangement continued and was manifested in various ways until Fred Paddock became vicar of Holy Trinity in the early 1960s.

As was St. James, Holy Trinity was obviously geographically close to St. John the Baptist, which may have been named after Stapylton's father's parish in England. The Montclair church was established in January 1888 and was demolished in the first quarter of the 20th century. (Holy Trinity's vestry minutes from 1914 remark that "St. John's is going to ruin.") It was a Gothic-style building constructed of both brick and wood, T-shaped, painted white with a red and white roof, with a belfry and bell on top. Although this claim stretches the imagination, a letter owned by the Lake County Historical Society states that Frank E. Wilson, a country boy of about 16 with no training whatsoever, drew up the plans for St. John's and constructed nearly all of the facility himself. The letter was written by sisters Mabel Millard McCullough and Minnie Millard Whitner, neighbors of Wilson's. Building of the facility was made possible by a prominent New York doctor, Egbert Guernsey, whose son, also a doctor, was an alcoholic; they moved to Montclair for a quieter life. When the church was torn down, a few of its furnishings were given to St. James, and portions of the lumber were used to build a home in Fruitland Park. The brass plaque honoring Julian's memory was placed at Holy Trinity.

The Yalaha and Corley Island churches are also no longer in existence.

While the other churches were in reasonable proximity to each other, St. John's in Brooksville was an exception. This parish, still going strong, is in Hernando County, about 35 miles from Leesburg as the crow flies. In July 1890 Julian was allowed by Bishop Weed to give up traveling there and spend more time in Chetwynd provided that Holy Trinity could increase his annual wage to $200. The stipend was raised by subscription.

Generally speaking, Holy Trinity has operated continuously since its inception but literally not quite so. The church was closed for several months at a time during the early years of the 1890s, possibly because of hot weather, maybe to give Julian a vacation as a job benefit, and perhaps due to his increasing health issues. In fact, the vestry minutes of June 19, 1891, quoting a Mr. Porter from Leesburg who proposed an August and September shutdown that year, which did take place, say this was "to allow Rev. J. E. Julian to take a holiday," and the vestry concurred that he "required a rest."

Furthermore, the journals of the Diocese of Florida indicate that J. J. Andrew was a missionary priest for Chetwynd and Montclair in 1891. It is possible he came in to help Julian.

In 1892, at age 52 and after a prolonged encounter with tuberculosis, Julian committed suicide. He was interred in the cemetery at Holy Trinity.

The following year a gravestone was erected over Julian's plot. In a description that appeared in The Leesburg Commercial, Stapylton wrote, "The whole monument, which was subscribed for by friends, is a beautiful piece of work and is a fitting memorial to a man whose calling away has left a void in the hearts of his people that will be difficult for his successor to fill. He has 'laid the foundation' and it is left for another to build thereon."

In an address in 1894, Bishop Weed paid tribute to Julian. "His life speaks for itself . . . (it) was full of good works," Weed said. "His untiring devotion made people love him. He was always at hand to comfort and aid the afflicted and distressed. One could write his epitaph in a few words: An unselfish man. His death has been a sore grief to me. I loved him, admired him, and respected him. I had perfect confidence in him as a Christian man, and this confidence has not been changed by his unfortunate end. May his soul rest in peace."

Joseph Julian's grave, 1894. Note the fence, the eastern boundary of the "church acre."

Julian's wife, Sarah E. Brewster Julian, remained in Leesburg the rest of her life. The daughter of a family of great wealth in Hudson, Ohio, she taught Sunday School at St. James and was that church's superintendent for years. She was recruited by Frank Cooke to be the first Leesburg librarian, a position she held until she was 84 years old. Cooke not only provided space in a building he owned but paid her salary. When the library eventually outgrew this space, it was relocated to the new Leesburg Women's Club in 1922. She died in 1936 and is buried next to her husband.

In October 1891, Joseph Julian attached the following note to an annual statement of the vestry. It provides food for thought for members of Holy Trinity even today.

"While cordially endorsing the above statement of the Vestry, and earnestly approving of it in every particular, commending it to careful and prayerful consideration, I will, as your Pastor, add but a word of exhortation.

"My plea, to every one who has been baptized into the church and confirmed, is to have you not only THINK of the solemn vows you have made, but to carry those vows into practice. You owe it to yourself, to the church, and to God, that you attend as regularly as possible the means of Grace in the House of God. Let not trifles ever keep you away from the services. It is a duty, not only a privilege, to meet with God's children, in God's house, to receive the blessings He promised to bestow there. Hoping and praying that the call of the Vestry and my earnest appeal to you will not be in vain, I remain,

"Your affectionate pastor,

"J.E. JULIAN"

Diocesan Affiliations

As might be expected as the state became more developed, Holy Trinity has gone through several—four, to be exact—diocesan affiliations.

At first the church was part of the Diocese of Florida, which covered the whole state and was officially formed in January 1838 with a total of just seven congregations. This diocese didn't elect its first bishop until 1851.

The Rt. Rev. Edwin Gardner Weed

Due to significant growth, the diocese was reorganized and officially incorporated in 1881. Its seat was in St. Augustine, and it was under the leadership of Bishop John Freeman Young at the time. Young was the second bishop of the diocese. Upon his death in 1885, he was succeeded by the Rev. Edwin

Gardner Weed, who had been a rector in Augusta, Ga. Holy Trinity associated with Weed during its founding period.

Almost immediately upon consecration, Weed began journeying throughout the state, reaching Key West before Episcopalians there even knew they had a new bishop, and travel became a major part of his life thereafter. It's been reported that he was on the road as much as eight weeks at a time, and in one of his early years as bishop he was home just 18 days.

At the beginning of his episcopate Weed had to deal with three large crises, including the Great Freeze of 1894-95 that destroyed the citrus industry in most of his diocese. None of these events prevented his ministering to the needy and establishing new missions. By the early 1890s, the number of new parishes and missions throughout Florida had grown to 110, too many for one bishop to handle. As a result, the General Convention of the Episcopal Church voted in 1892 to divide the diocese and create the Missionary Jurisdiction of South Florida; this new entity would then officially become the Diocese of South Florida in 1923.

Weed, who was known as the "missionary bishop" because over 77 missions were founded during his tenure, remained as head of the Diocese of Florida until he died in 1924. Under his direction, the diocesan seat was moved to Jacksonville in 1895.

Following his death, he was praised by contemporaries for his relationship with people and for his friendship and cheerfulness. "Perhaps the American Church has never before known a more approachable bishop," claimed the rector and wardens of St. John's in Jacksonville. Another diocesan clergyman said, "He was a shepherd who knew his sheep."

The website for St. Cyrian's Historic Episcopal Church in St. Augustine indicates that both Young and Weed were, to an extent, early civil rights activists.

"Bishop Young fought to regain the black membership (from before the Civil War) by developing educational programs for emancipated slaves," according to the site. "By the time he died in 1885, the Diocese had created nine African-American Episcopal Churches in north Florida.

"Bishop Weed ordained five black priests in Florida even though the Diocesan newspaper stated, 'We do not favor the ordination of colored men to the priesthood.'"

The Rt. Rev. William Crane Gray

At its inception, the Missionary Jurisdiction of South Florida had four parishes, 35 organized missions and 16 mission stations. (Stations had smaller memberships than did missions.) The jurisdiction was administered by the Rt. Rev. William Crane Gray, the bishop who worked with Holy Trinity in its formative years. He served until his retirement in 1913, making St. Luke's in Orlando his home church and, thus, the cathedral.

Gray had been a chaplain of a Tennessee regiment during the Civil War and was a priest in Nashville at the time of his consecration. He had a son who was once the rector of Grace Church in Ocala and later became the bishop of the Episcopal Diocese of Northern Indiana. Gray was living with the son at the time of his death in 1919.

Dorothy Paddock's 1976 history of Holy Trinity, "In the Beauty of Holiness," contains what she termed a "poignantly human" excerpt from Gray's diary that he wrote following a visit to Chetwynd in the summer of 1894. "A full set of services, Morning Prayer, Litany, Sermon, Confirmation and Holy Communion on the hottest day of the season, a hard day's work, none to assist me—my vestments wet with perspiration at the end of the services."

Holy Trinity remained in the Diocese of South Florida until 1969 when this diocese, also having become too large, was divided into three separate bodies, one being the church's current affiliate, the Diocese of Central Florida based in Orlando.

Progress ensues, then stalls

The few years immediately after Holy Trinity's consecration were marked by a time of steady growth.

The first wedding in the new church took place Sept. 28, 1889, between British subject Robert Bird of Lady Lake and Annie Palmer.

The first confirmation of record, of George Pybus, age 16, occurred June 24, 1894.

On a different note, the donation of the 14+ acres of the Tasker land happened during this interval also. So did the construction of one of the church's most notable features, the lych (rhymes with "ditch") gate which is in the south fence fronting Spring Lake Road.

Holy Trinity's rare lych gate.

Lych gates are often found in Anglican and European churchyards but are fairly rare in this country. Their purpose is to serve as a resting place for the casket and pall bearers before the priest meets and accompanies the funeral procession into the church or to the burial site. The current practice is for prayers to be said there with the family before the procession. ("Lich", from which the name comes, is Middle English for "corpse.")

Holy Trinity's lych gate was erected in 1889 and was funded by Emily Tatham. Interestingly, she didn't arrive in this country until May 1892. She then lived with her niece, Maya Schrieber, whom she had raised, and Maya's husband, Frederick. The Schriebers' daughter Emily Dorothy was baptized March 5, 1894, at Holy Trinity with Tatham and Villiers Chernocke Smith as sponsors. After the disastrous freeze the following winter, the Schriebers and Tatham moved to Ocala where she founded the Band of Mercy, an organization devoted to teaching children kindness and gentleness toward animals. Tatham was a life-long Quaker but worshiped regularly as an Episcopalian.

In 1889, the year of consecration at Holy Trinity, Christmas was on a Wednesday but the holiday service was held the following Sunday. According to the vestry minutes, "The church was tastefully decorated, and the Xmas service was held (today) instead of on the 25th, Mr. Julian being unable to come out on that day."

The following April, Bishop Weed reappointed Stapylton as senior warden of the vestry and Alexander Cazalet as junior warden. John Vickers-Smith replaced Thomas Vincent as secretary/treasurer.

According to minutes in December 1890, Jonathan Luther, a master local cabinetmaker and carpenter, was to make a chair for the chancel as well as a baptismal font. This seat was supposedly to be a bishop's chair, but there is no mention in the minutes of that. Luther had also crafted a prayer desk, possibly the lectern, and at least half the pews in the church; the remaining pews, and the other clerical chair, were constructed later as copies.

At the time he did this work, Luther and his wife, Maria Josephine, originally from Rhode Island, were members of this church and were among its founders. Sometime later they joined St. James in Leesburg before eventually moving on to Cordele, Ga.

A few of the items of liturgical altar brassware still in use today at Holy Trinity were obtained during this period. Among these items are an altar cross and Eucharistic candleholders that were contributed by English patrons and employed in services at the Vickers-Smith barn while the church was being built.

Altar hangings, clerical stoles and offering bags are other early furnishings, now displayed in shadow boxes on the interior walls. Most of these were embroidered by the Smith sisters—Margaret, Elizabeth, Sarah and Helen—the first three of whom were among the church's founders. All studied at the Royal School of Art Needlework in London and were the children of James and Mary Smith.

Shadowbox with altar hanging and offering bags.

In October, 1891, the vestry prepared a leaflet which was essentially a stewardship letter. Apparently the church at that time operated on a fiscal year ending September 30. This letter states that 42 services had been held during the fiscal year with averages of 29 in the congregation and 10 for communion. (No one could receive the sacrament unless confirmed.) Total expenses were $265, which included $200 for Julian's stipend, a $30 diocesan assessment, $12 for cleaning the church and $23 for sundry items such as oil, matches and sacramental wine. "Subscriptions ranging from $2.50 to $15.00 per annum" were not enough to cover anticipated expenses. In addition other needed improvements were cited.

The vestry wrote, "When it is remembered that practically the whole cost of the church was defrayed by friends in England, it will be conceded that the least that can be expected of us, the beneficiaries of this generous gift, is to show ourselves worthy of it in the heartiness of our maintenance of the church and our support of its services."

Julian then added his note which appears earlier at the end of the section about him.

Within less than 12 months Julian would be dead. Almost certainly this tragedy shook the congregation. He was followed by a number of men, mainly supply priests or missionaries, who served for brief periods. There would not be much stability in the ministerial position at Holy Trinity until well after the turn of the century. In the meantime, as might be expected, growth slowed and survival of the church and maintenance of the building became urgent issues.

Two changes were made to the vestry in 1892 with Louis Bosanquet and George Pybus coming on board.

In 1893 the vestry voted to subscribe a $90 share in the Leesburg Savings and Loan for the purpose of joining Leesburg and Montclair in raising funds to build a rectory next to St. James.

Stapylton served as lay reader for about 14 months from June 1894 until August 1895. By the time his service ended, he had moved to Leesburg and discontinued his subscription.

As ominous as all this may have been, it was minor in comparison to events that happened just a few months before.

The Great Freeze

The year 1894 was, of course, a time before NOAA, Doppler radar and mass communication, so there was really no indication that any big problem was coming.

The citrus industry was in a very prosperous condition by then. Growers were making lots of money and, in turn, reinvesting in new and larger groves.

Christmas Day of that year was sunny and beautiful with temperatures in the 80s. But three days later a strong cold front from the northwest brought a heavy rainstorm and high winds to the area; by the next morning the temperature had dropped to anywhere from 12 to 18 degrees. The entire year's citrus crop, most of it still hanging on the trees, was killed during this three-day cataclysm.

It's not as if the area hadn't faced adversity before. There had been a substantial earlier freeze in January 1886. At that time Augustus Bosanquet noted, "Temperatures dipped below 20 degrees each night [at his home, Fair Oaks.] Memorable blizzard from the Northwest; trees lost all leaves; fruit frozen and wood three to five feet frozen." This event was followed by a moderate hurricane that July and influenza epidemics from 1886 into 1889.

Frank Cooke wrote to his father after the post-Christmas freeze. "We have just had a most disastrous frost," he said. "Last night the thermometer went down to about 16 degrees and consequently all the unshipped orange crop, estimated at about 2 ¾ million boxes, has been *entirely* destroyed, and the only question now is whether the trees are hurt although the general opinion is that they are.

"The outlook in this section is most serious. I supposed at least 75% of the crop in the neighborhood was being held for a better market and so are all destroyed and what we are all going to do until the next crop comes in a year's time without any money I don't know. It seems to be perfectly useless to hope that the reports are exaggerated, but I hope they may be. I have never seen a bluer or a sicker lot of people in my life."

The fruits of the Great Freeze—devastation.

Following this freeze, the worst thing that could have happened next did. January 1895 brought warm, wet weather which promoted new growth in the trees. They lost their leaves and also became engorged with sap as they fought to survive. The presence of so much sap set up the trees for a knockout punch in round two in early February.

Louis Bosanquet recorded a 12-degree reading at Fair Oaks during this second freeze. The result, said Dorothy Paddock in her book, was that the trees "literally exploded, with the sounds of their cracking and splitting limbs and boughs echoing over the desolate landscape."

The same thing occurred in many other places throughout much of Florida. According to agricultural extension agent Henry Swenson in his book "Countdown for Agriculture in Orange County, Florida," as quoted in the Orlando Sentinel, "When the second freeze hit on Feb. 7, people who were here then said they heard the trees pop like pistol shots as freezing sap split the bark."

This freeze, which also lasted three days, killed a high percentage of the trees, 90% or more by some estimates. By differing accounts it took the industry until somewhere between 1910 to 1919 to completely recover, and this event marked the start of a gradual southward migration by orange growers.

Frank Cooke noted that growers in this immediate area lost 12,000 boxes of citrus at $2 a box – a lot of money in 1895.

The Sentinel reported that the total number of boxes shipped from Florida dropped from five million the previous year to 147,000 after the freeze with virtually all of it coming from the extreme southern part of the state.

Paddock wrote, "This has been regarded by some historians as 'the greatest natural disaster to occur in the United States up to that time.'"

In his book "Pioneer Trails of Lake County," William F. Gouveria claimed that after the Great Freeze people survived on rabbits, turtles and cabbage. He also said that budwood to rebud the sprouts was scarce.

Many residents of Chetwynd fled in panic.

Alfred Bosanquet, a nephew of Augustus, had this recollection. "I remember as a child growing up and seeing some of the houses still standing, with the breakfast dishes on the table, the blankets on the beds, the windows pulled down, but the doors unlocked," he said. "The people had gotten discouraged on seeing their groves and all the fruit frozen and caught the first train out. They didn't even pack up their silver on the table."

Chetwynd disappeared from railroad and Rand McNally maps.

Where did those residents go?

They moved to a variety of locations—some back to England and others to such places as Vancouver, Portland, Toronto, Boston, Savannah, Nebraska and Asheville, N.C.

Fortunately some remained. These were, in the main, people with the financial resources and ingenuity to diversify their crops. They kept Holy Trinity afloat during this very difficult period when many other churches went under.

The historic churchyard

For being such quiet, low-key places, cemeteries are usually sites of interest and sometimes of mystery. Holy Trinity's is no exception.

An example: The oldest grave in the yard, at first blush, appears to be that of Beverly Hail Luther, son of cabinetmaker Jonathan Luther and wife Josephine, who died in 1882, four years before the church came into existence. His stone is odd in that it lies flat and is quite ornate, totally out of character with the rest. His is the only grave in the cemetery that faces east in the Anglican tradition. All others point west. Logic and the fact that the inscription reads "in memory of" lead to the likelihood that the stone is a memorial to Beverly Luther, placed at a somewhat later date. But no written record exists to prove this theory.

The first burial recorded in the church register was that of James Smith, a reclamation engineer from Portsmouth, England, and the father of John Vickers-Smith. James died before the church was constructed but after services had started at other locations and the building site had been determined. Apparently he and, slightly later, his wife, Mary, were first buried in the original church acre. At some point after use of the current cemetery began around 1894, about the time that Holy Trinity received the Tasker Land, the Smiths were re-interred. Their graves are now next to their daughters Elizabeth, Sarah and Margaret, who all died in the 1920's, as well as son John and others of his family.

Mary Smith was one of five deaths recorded in the parish register of St. James in Leesburg; her burial was indicated as being at Chetwynd. Two others, brothers Arthur W.S. Perkins and Stanley A. Perkins of Groton, Conn., who passed away in 1894, are identified in the St. James parish register as "2 young men from the north died in Fla. of T.B. several hours apart. Both buried in same grave."

A person walking through the yard will obviously see some of the surnames mentioned so far in this book but not as many early-member graves as might be expected. Most of the burials have occurred over the past 50 years.

Holy Trinity churchyard.

A $4,000 bequest left in 1933 by Louise Bosanquet helped appreciably in the upkeep of the churchyard. She designated this money specifically for cemetery maintenance. Years later a Perpetual Care Fund was established for the yard.

Cremations have become much more common in recent years with the blessing of the Episcopal Church. Two locations are available for the burial of cremains. As quoted directly from Holy Trinity's Perpetual Care Policy, "The outside perimeter beyond the Good Shepherd statue are for cremains, whether in an urn, box, or buried in the ground . . . The section around the Good Shepherd statue and bordered by sidewalks is reserved for individual cremains mixed with soil from around the statue."

Among the more notable graves in the yard, along with Julian's, are those of the Rev. Fred Paddock, who led the church through its period of greatest development in the 1960s and '70s and who is discussed in considerable detail later in this book, and William Reed Newell (1868-1956).

Newell was a noted evangelist, Bible teacher and later assistant superintendent at the Moody Bible Institute in Chicago. While on his way to teach a class one day, he wrote the lyrics for the hymn "On Calvary" after meditating about Christ's suffering at Calvary and all that it meant to him. A friend and colleague, Daniel Brink Towner, musical director at the Institute, composed the music. The hymn was first published in 1895.

Newell's son David McCheyne Newell (1898-1986) and his wife, Frances Bosanquet (1892-1969), are also buried in the cemetery as are various other members of the Newell family and five additional church clergy besides Julian and Paddock: Randolph Blackford, Herbert Edson Covell, Lloyd Ashley Cox, Paul Heckters and Ogden Ludlow.

David Newell was a well-known author whose stories and drawings appeared in a variety of newspapers and sports magazines throughout the country. According to online encyclopedia Wikipedia, he was "perhaps most famous for his books regarding early twentieth century life in western central Florida." In many of his writings, he dealt with the desirability of Lake County as a sportsman's mecca, creating a considerable amount of favorable publicity for the area. The younger Newell was editor of Field and Stream magazine for several years, hosted a nature and hunting show on television in the 1950s, accompanied Annie Oakley on some hunting trips before her death in 1926, and was a friend of noted Florida author Marjorie Kinnan Rawlings. Furthermore, he was an illustrator whose art appeared in dozens of publications. Many of his paintings can now be seen at the Leesburg Heritage Museum.

The churchyard also contains a fairly large number of graves of veterans from the Spanish-American War through Vietnam and one of a teenager, Brittany Anne May, who was killed during the Groundhog Day Tornado in 2007.

In addition, the vestry designated a section for cremated pets in 2009.

Part 2: 1895-1960

The Dark Age

LITTLE INFORMATION about Holy Trinity is available from any source for approximately 20 years following the Great Freeze of 1894-95, thus the name chosen for this period.

As previously stated, the populations of Chetwynd and of Holy Trinity Church dropped dramatically following the freeze. Only a small number of church members remained and were responsible for keeping the facility afloat. Even in conjunction with St. James, Holy Trinity was unable to support a regular minister so was served for a number of years by supply priests and missionaries, many of whom stayed for just short intervals.

Holy Trinity, St. James and the other churches he served had indeed been fortunate to have Julian's services, even for such a brief period. A note in William Crane Gray's journal in 1890 (before he became bishop), reads, "It is my calculation that each missionary has had three men's work to do. How this is to be rectified is a problem well worth your consideration. The lack of clergy is a serious difficulty which is becoming more serious every day because the people are getting together in little hamlets and in the new rapidly growing towns and forming new congregations and asking for this bread of life. A few years ago, when our present secretary of the Board of Missions was at work in the lake region about Eustis, there was not a church building in many miles. Now in that very district we have churches at Chetwynd, Montclair, Leesburg, Eustis, Pittman, Lane Park, and Zellwood."

There were indications that Holy Trinity might have problems with the priest's stipend even before the freeze. The vestry minutes of May 19, 1893, specify that Bishop Weed had asked for a guaranteed stipend; the church could commit $112 a year but needed $200.

Although the building was quite new, it still required upkeep. Minutes for August 1893 mention that the roof had been fixed, the chancel floor stained, and "locks and door fasteners" had been repaired. Less than two years later, the record of Feb. 23, 1895, shows that E.W. Kline had submitted a bid to replace the roof for $135 and to paint the facility for $35. The church purchased a horse and buggy for clergyman A. Kinney Hall that October from an outlay that was probably split with St. James. These acquisitions remained the property of Holy Trinity.

The March 30, 1895, minutes indicate that the congregation couldn't maintain its stipend and asked if Mr. (J. Charles) Kimball, the priest at the time, would continue. The record also states that Stapylton was moving to Leesburg and must drop his subscription to Chetwynd, adding, "I suppose Budd will do the same." In addition, it was made clear that the congregation could not afford more than $150 a year for a rector.

Gray's journal a few years after his consecration as bishop notes, "A number of places once flourishing and in a prosperous condition are now diminished by the exodus after the calamity of the freeze." He added that most places were "poorly prepared to sustain the financial requirements of even occasional services of the church, owing to their personal struggle for a bare living."

A highlight of the latter years of this decade was a dedication in June 1897 of the brass missal stand in honor of the "Diamond Jubilee of Her Britannic Majesty, Queen Victoria." The money for this stand was raised through subscription. Inscribed "Holy Trinity Mission, Chetwynd, Florida," the stand is in use to this day.

Joseph M. McGrath was the priest at that time. He served St. James and St. John's in addition to Holy Trinity.

The Rev. Joseph M. McGrath

St. John's Church, MONTCLAIR.

Ash-Wedne-day.
Evenso-g, with Address.................. 7.30 P. M.
Sundays.
1st Sunday, Evens-ng with Sermon...... 7.30 P. M.
2 1 Sunday, Litany and Holy Commun-
ion.................... .... 8.30 A. M.
3d and 4th Sundays, Evensong, with
Sermon............ .... 7.30 P. M.
Week-Days. Including Holy Week.
Evensong, Litany and Meditation,
Wednesday at .... 7.30 P. M.
Easter Day.
Matins, Sermon and The Holy Eucha-
rist......... .... 8.00 A. M.
Children's Festival,...................... 3.00 P. M.
Low Easter.
Evensong and Sermon................... 7.30 P. M.

Holy Trinity Church, CHETWYND.

Week-Days, Including Holy Week.
Fridays, Litany and Address............ 7.30 P. M.
Sundays.
2d Sunday, Litany, Sermon and Holy
Communion........................... 11.00 A. M.
Evensong and Sermon other Sundays 3.00 P. M.
Easter Day
Evensong and Sermon................... 3.00 P. M.
Low Easter.
Matins, Sermon and Holy Eucharist...10.30 A. M.

Lent, 1897.

DEARLY BELOVED :

AGAIN Holy Church calls upon her children to keep "The dear Feast of Lent." It is a call to a closer walk with Him who loves us. Surely each one of us as far as possible will come to this Feast which He has prepared for us :

"The love of Jesus what it is
None but His loved ones know."

Let us come apart and rest with Him awhile.

Rules for Keeping Lent.

1st. Attend if possible every service of the Church, and receive the Holy Communion as often as it is celebrated.

2d. Give some portion of your time each day to self-examination, meditation, prayer and Bible study.

3d. Practice self-denial and give the proceeds of your self-denial as an offering on Easter-Day to Him who freely gave Himself for you.

4th. If thy brother have aught against thee be reconciled to thy brother.

5th. Abstain from light reading and all world-ly amusements, and give the time thus saved to good words and works.

6th. Try to bring some one with you to each service.

7th. Lay aside if possible each day something for your Easter offering.

My prayer for you daily shall be that on Easter Day and on all the days that peace and joy which the world can neither give nor take away may be yours.

Faithfully Your Friend,
J. M. McGRATH.

1897 church flyer

The Spanish-American War, the first armed conflict since the founding of the church, began in April 1898. Senior warden Villiers Chernocke Smith, still a British citizen, enlisted in the service.

The vestry minutes of May 27, 1898, again deal with problems with the stipend, mention the current priest, James Neville Thompson, and note, "Subscribers had left and others talking of leaving." After that there are no more entries for more than 16 years.

Not surprisingly Thompson also rode circuit. He had responsibilities for the missions in Chetwynd, Leesburg, Montclair, Brooksville (which must have been "added back" after Julian's death), and Lake Buddy in southeastern Lake County.

As if the Great Freeze wasn't bad enough, a subsequent freeze in February 1899 might have had a worse impact

The Rev. James Neville Thompson

except that many trees were already dead. However, the second calamity did wipe out any work growers had done since 1895. Louis Bosanquet recorded in his register, "Temperature at 15 degrees, fruit frozen, trees killed, severe freeze; the fountain in Mote's Garden was frozen solid; on the 15th snow on the veranda; one of the worst freezes on record."

The temperature dropped to minus 2 in Tallahassee, the only time a below zero reading has ever been recorded in Florida.

By 1901 the demise of the Bucket and Dipper Club marked yet another indication of the dire situation in Chetwynd/Fruitland Park. Ninety-five men had belonged to this group over the course of its existence but only 15, according to local public records, remained in the area after the Great Freeze of 1894-95, and just a dozen were left in the organization in 1900.

Dorothy Paddock's "In the Beauty of Holiness" states, "In 1901, the congregation is listed as forty members with total receipts of $127.48." About 15 of those members were children.

Holy Trinity certainly wasn't unusual in having such a small membership at that time. Records show that in the diocese in 1899 there were 60 churches serving a grand total of 2,322 people, an average of just under 39 persons per location. The figure of 39 is a little misleading, though. Only about half a dozen of the churches were parishes (the rest being missions) and these were much more sizable, somewhat skewing the average. Grace in Ocala, for instance, had about 200 members.

The Rev. Clarence M. Frankel

Clarence M. Frankel, a missionary, served Holy Trinity from 1902-1905. He was divorced prior to arriving here; his ex-wife then wed an Episcopal priest in Baltimore who had accepted a call to a parish near Philadelphia. The bishop of that diocese refused to recognize that priest's marriage and forced the parish to withdraw the call. A story about this matter made the front page of the New York Times. No information is available as to whether Holy Trinity or this diocese knew about Frankel's divorce or, if so, whether it was of concern.

Anecdotes involving two other priests from this period may be of interest.

Aykroyd Stoney, who served from 1908-1911, was born in England to a family of butchers. Having served in his late teens as an apprentice butcher himself, he was a Methodist minister in Newfoundland, Canada, before eventually coming here. According to reports, he was once observed drinking 13 cups of tea at an after-church social at the Bosanquet residence.

The Rev. George Henry Ward

George Henry Ward, priest from 1912 to 1921 was said to have leanings toward the Greek Orthodox Church and consequently strung bells over the communion rail at Holy Trinity. He served until age 82 when he resigned because of increasing blindness as well as age.

Ernest Davis, rector many years later (1985-1991), told a story of the period not involving clergy: "Soon after I arrived here, the Diocesan Historian sent around a list of the churches in the diocese, ranked by the dates of their foundation. And Holy Trinity, Fruitland Park, was listed as being organized around 1910. Holy Trinity was originally named Holy Trinity Church, Chetwynd, not Fruitland Park. Since the Diocesan records list churches by location, after it no longer made sense to call this location Chetwynd since there was no longer a post office here, 'Chetwynd, Holy Trinity' disappeared from the list and 'Fruitland Park, Holy Trinity' appeared. Sometime after that, someone made up a list of churches and must have assumed that the Chetwynd church went out of existence, and that the Fruitland Park church came into existence at the same time, without realizing that they were describing the same church!"

In 1913, the diocese had to write off an assessment of $25 due from Holy Trinity, but Bishop Gray reported that there were "good congregations" during his visits to the church in January and April.

The following year, Holy Trinity listed 25 communicants.

Without documentation, it is only speculation as to what else may have occurred during this period. It seems likely, however, that by shortly after the turn of the century a small but perhaps stabilizing congregation spent the next 10-15 years with limited funds just holding services and maintaining the building and property.

The Winter Colony and the beginning of a boom

Although the earliest residents of Fruitland Park came here to grow citrus, some rapidly discovered that there was money to be made in other ways from the area's winter climate. Entrepreneurs like Granville Chetwynd-Stapylton became involved in development projects and railroad introduction with an eye toward bringing in more people to profit from citrus. But by 1888, the town began to draw seasonal residents of some means who came not to grow fruit but to socialize, recreate and escape the snow. As it increased in size this group, collectively, became known as "the Winter Colony."

The first members were Dr. and Mrs. Eben Alden of Rockland, Maine. They, in turn, persuaded some other folks from their state to come to Fruitland Park.

In 1892, Mr. and Mrs. W.T. Dean from Holyoke, Massachusetts, began spending time in this area. They then inspired other residents of their hometown to do likewise, in particular William and Minnie Dwight, who would play a significant role in Holy Trinity's history for many years.

Shortly after the Aldens arrived, Mr. and Mrs. George T. Clark came from the Chicago area and they attracted others from the Windy City.

George Clark was a member of a family that was substantially connected with the development of this area. He was the son of architect Jonathan Clark who had visited Florida about two years before. An early settler in Chicago, Jonathan was one of the city's largest contractors erecting, among other buildings, the famous Art

Institute on Michigan Avenue. His sons were listed in the 1900 Cook County, Ill., census as having the same occupation.

Jonathan was so pleased with this locality on his visit that he purchased a tract of land from the town's founder, Orlando P. Rooks, who was to clear and plant it.

Two years later Jonathan returned and brought George with him. Both men soon were involved in varying capacities with two stores in Fruitland Park.

Jonathan, in addition, acquired several other pieces of property, most of which were used to plant citrus. But on one of the tracts, on Mirror Lake, he built, with the help of another son, John Yates, a winter home he named Palm Villa.

Jonathan died in 1902. At that time John Yates Clark came to reside in Fruitland Park permanently for several years before moving to Leesburg. Before his death in 1928, John Clark would engage in many pursuits in Leesburg—running an automobile business, establishing the Light and Water Plant, being president of a company, and serving on the city council and the chamber of commerce.

George Clark went on to build the Gardenia Hotel (on Berckman between Rose and College) in 1907. By 1913 he had become the sole owner of the hotel as well as the owner of Palm Villa. In 1914 he constructed the casino, a large facility that included a stage, dressing rooms, running water, electricity and heat that would be used for a variety of community gatherings and entertainments for many years. To a much lesser extent, the building is still employed for some of the same purposes to this day.

The Casino, Fruitland Park, Florida

George, who died in 1918, was married to Ida Goodridge. While the Clarks apparently didn't belong to Holy Trinity, Ida and other Goodridges were active in the church. Many from that family (other than her and her husband) are buried in the cemetery. A sister Nellie, with whom Ida lived and grew citrus following the deaths of both sisters' spouses, was the church's choir director in the 1920s. Another sister, Carrie, was the first women's guild president. Carrie married Elisha Wightman, the postmaster of Fruitland Park, who was also a member of Holy Trinity. Interestingly, Elisha was the brother of lumberman Elias who was Nellie's husband. Elias died in 1895 and is buried in Wisconsin.

By the fall of 1913 a company called the Lake County Land Owners Association had formed to promote the sale of real estate and, in the process, to increase the size of Fruitland Park and Lady Lake. (Although the latter town wasn't incorporated until 1925, its name goes back to the early 1880s as noted in the Lady Lake Historical Society's 2011 book, "The Story of Lady Lake.")

Ormund Powers wrote an article called "Slick Salesmen Helped Cities Grow at Turn of Century" for the June 30, 1999, edition of the Orlando Sentinel. In it, he called the association "a high-pressure organization of never-say-die salesmen."

Lillian Vickers-Smith saw things differently in her "History of Fruitland Park" which was written while the group was still in existence. She claimed, "This organization has done much for the Park . . . It has put in many clay roads, donated land to worthy causes, and has always been ready to help in all progressive movements."

Powers drew on an interview that Ben Collier, an early resident and eventual land salesman, had with the Lake County Historical Society some years prior.

Collier talked about the company's pricing practices. "When the land company first started, they tried to sell the land for $35 per acre," he said, "but normal people wouldn't buy it. They put the price up to $100 per acre, and it went like hot cakes."

He explained that officers of the association first bought 20,000 acres and divided it into 10-acre plots. Investors got a building lot in town with every 10 acres they bought. The association promoted this offer in a number of large-circulation newspapers in the north and in several leading magazines.

Prospective buyers in groups of anywhere from a dozen to 40 came down from the north by train, staying for several days, usually at the Gardenia Hotel, until they were sold or decided against buying. "But most of those people always bought because we had some mighty good salesmen," Collier said.

He continued, "About the best salesman was J.T. Lloyd. One day I brought in a prospect, and Lloyd sold him 10 acres. When the man went to pay, he took out a wallet and pulled off nine $100 bills.

"There were quite a few more bills in there. Lloyd saw them and said, 'What you need is 20 acres.' So he made a deal and gave him an extra discount and sold him 20 acres. The man didn't have enough money in that pocketbook, so he reached and got another pocketbook and paid him, and there was still lots of money left. Before the man left the office, he had bought 40 acres and paid all cash for it."

Dr. William Alexander MacKenzie was one of the men most responsible for the establishment of the Land Owners Association. He became its president.

MacKenzie, well regarded in this area, ministered extensively to the sick during an influenza epidemic in 1917, was honored by President Woodrow Wilson for his medical work during World War I, played a key role in the development of a large grape industry in the region, served three terms in the state legislature, and was in his tenth consecutive term as Leesburg's mayor when he died in 1929.

It was he who donated the lot for Holy Trinity's (women's) guild house.

The Bosanquets

The Bosanquets are perhaps the most storied family associated with Holy Trinity. Members of this family played key roles in the church from its founding until 1992.

Originally from near London and of French Huguenot origins, Augustus and Eugene, two of Percival and Louise Bevan Bosanquet's six sons, were the first to arrive in this area. The father, who had close ties with the Crown, was a merchant with the East Indian Trading Company. Like most others who ventured to Florida at that time, Augustus and Eugene came to grow citrus. Interestingly, all six of the boys, two of whom died very young, had their father's first name—Percival—as their middle name. Those who survived to adulthood were well educated, Augustus at Cambridge University and the rest at Eton College.

Between Augustus and Eugene, the former, born in 1860, was more prominent in Holy Trinity's history. Augustus bought 100 acres on Zephyr Lake from freed slave Martin Tanner and proceeded to build a two-story, 11-room mansion. This house, which he named Fair Oaks, was closely associated with church events for many years thereafter. Reportedly he had a saw mill set up on site to cut the massive pines used for the foundation and the wood for the walls and floors. He and Eugene also set out 20 acres of oranges along with their specialty, mandarins, and raised many other plants with seeds they had brought with them from England. Among these was a peach called Red Ceylon which at the time was the most tropical peach grown in Florida.

Fair Oaks

Eugene died early in 1892 of a rattlesnake bite incurred while hunting near Daytona Beach. Little else is known about him except that in 1886 he bought a half acre of land near his brother for $30 and that he worked at a Daytona hotel a couple of years before his death.

Son number three, Louis, born in 1865, came to this area in 1888 to join his older brothers. He went on to play a very important part in Holy Trinity's history. About five years after Louis' arrival, Augustus turned Fair Oaks over to him and left the U.S. to become Secretary of the Royal British Club in Lisbon, Portugal. Unmarried, Augustus eventually returned to his family's home in England and died there in 1930.

Louis Percival Bosanquet

Louis married Ellen Lewis Hall Nov. 4, 1891. She was from Marietta, Ohio, but was the daughter of John and Frances Ellen Hereford Hall of Fruitland Park. Interestingly, Ellen was a direct descendant of Betty Washington Hall, the sister of George Washington. Since she was an American, it is rumored that their marriage was not particularly well received by Louis' family. An anecdote about their courtship concerns Ellen riding her horse to Fair Oaks in the early morning hours to flirt with him as he looked out the upstairs window in his nightshirt.

She would prove to be a valuable member of Holy Trinity and Fruitland Park in her own right, holding key positions in several church and community organizations.

Louis and Ellen had three children—Frances, Louise and Alfred—born in that order during the 1890s.

Following the Great Freeze of 1894-95 and the subsequent freeze of 1899, only a few determined and financially secure families stayed, the Bosanquets among them.

Much of Louis' stability at the time was due to his diversified plantings. He owned a collection of botanical books, one dating to 1595. While most of the remaining fruit growers were farming common produce, he began to cultivate a variety of trees and bushes.

For instance, he planted, to the north of his house, a formal English garden and an expanse of antique roses of perhaps 75 types. The roses were sold, both at the home and at a family-owned floral shop in Leesburg, for weddings and other occasions. North of the flowers grew acres of watermelons. According to a story written by Lee King in the Oct. 15, 2000, Orlando Sentinel, "on any summer afternoon, one could stroll from one end of the second floor porch to the other and have their eyes drenched in the dazzling rich hues from Mother Nature's palate."

Eventually the Fair Oaks estate contained about 1,000 varieties of trees and plants including 14 types of bamboo, about the same number of palms, a large quantity of hibiscus from Hawaii, and some experimental plants shipped from the U.S. Department of Agriculture.

In addition, Louis developed hybrid crinums with the best known, and possibly the most popular, being introduced commercially in 1930. Called *Crinum x Ellen Bosanquet*, it is a beautiful magenta lily named for his wife. He also created one named for himself, the *Louis Bosanquet Crinum*, a small pale pink or pink lavender plant.

Lillian Vickers-Smith wrote about his efforts in her book, "The History of Fruitland Park:" "It is his knowledge of horticulture that makes the spacious grounds of Bosanquet Place one of the most interesting and beautiful in Florida."

Three Bosanquets served as senior wardens at the church over the years. Louis held that position for six years, his son Alfred for 19 years and his grandson Gershon for three.

Fair Oaks is located southeast of the church on a single track dirt road going south off Spring Lake Road just to the east of a large apartment complex. Since this property is near Holy Trinity, one of the men routinely checked the church for fires after a typical Central Florida thunderstorm.

The vestry cited Louis following his death on April 19, 1930, about a month after his brother Augustus died. Louis had been a vestry member since May 10, 1893, and, as senior warden or as secretary, had attended every meeting of that group until his passing. Louis was remembered for his "constant support in every way, his untiring efforts for the upbuilding of the Mission and its proper management and maintenance. Without him it would hardly have survived the disastrous days of the Big Freeze; without him it might have become but another of the abandoned churches of South Florida but with the earnest support of a few devoted communicants he carried it successfully through to better days. One of his chief joys lay in the well-being and well-doing of Holy Trinity. We sorely miss him but his example remains as an inspiration."

An English custom of holding teas after Sunday afternoon church services began with the founding of the English Colony. Except for a few years during World War II, the teas were held at Fair Oaks until they were largely discontinued in the early 1960s. These were sit-down social affairs on the front lawn. According to Dorothy Paddock's book, "Many local residents, by no means all of them Episcopalians, remember coming out to attend the afternoon services as children and young people, often walking the several miles from Fruitland Park, then enjoying the delicious cakes and sandwiches at 'Bosanquets' Place.'"

Whenever the bishop attended a high tea, guests made every effort to exhibit perfect English manners. A deviation from this protocol occurred once when a lady stood to speak and her underwear suddenly fell to her ankles. Everyone gasped in shock except for her daughter nearby. "Mama, I told you not to wear the panties with the shot elastic!" she exclaimed. Her mother was mortified, ran into the house and didn't come out until the bishop left.

On occasion, other church-related activity took place at Fair Oaks. During the 1920s, at least one bazaar was held there to benefit Holy Trinity. And in January 1948 a "Gay '90s Parade" was staged on the property to raise funds to assist St. James with its renovation after a fire in 1947. Over 300 guests attended that event, bringing in about $800.

Dorothy Paddock cited another example of Bosanquet hospitality: "Early in the (1940s), even before war had been declared by the United States, there were Royal Air Force Officers in training at a base near Lakeland. Nearly every week, members of the squadron would spend their Sundays at Fair Oaks, attending church at Holy Trinity, enjoying a typical British meal with the family, and surely relishing a genuine touch of home in this southern atmosphere."

High Tea at Fair Oaks

Paddock added, "Out of the dozen or so young men included in this group, only one survived the war."

Louis and Ellen's older daughter, Frances, married sportsman and author David McCheyne Newell. The Newells had three daughters. Betty Washington (d. 1926) and Nancy Ayers (d. 2000) are buried with their parents in the churchyard, and Priscilla Bevan is living in Vermont as of this writing.

Alfred Bosanquet Family

Standing left to right: Jeanne Marie Bosanquet Gilchrist, Gershon Percival Bosanquet, Frances Louise Bosanquet Couch Simpson, Louis Percival Bosanquet, Blanche Ward Bosanquet Knowles, with their parents, Alfred Percival Bosanquet and Ruth Marion Ward Bosanquet on their 50th wedding anniversary, October 1, 1975.

Louise Bosanquet, Louis and Ellen's younger daughter, died in 1933, leaving the $4,000 bequest for cemetery maintenance previously mentioned. This legacy, still in trust, was a godsend to address an ongoing problem and formed the basis for the present Perpetual Care Fund.

Son Alfred served with an ambulance unit attached to the Fifth French Division in World War I and participated in three major and four minor offensives. Senior warden at Holy Trinity from 1930-1947, he and his son notified the Leesburg Fire Department upon seeing the St. James fire. Alfred married Ruth Ward (no relation to the former Holy Trinity priest) in 1925 in Missouri. They had five children: three daughters, Blanche Ward, Jeanne Marie and Frances Louise, and two sons, Louis and Gershon, both of whom carried the traditional family middle name of Percival. Blanche, Jeanne, Frances and Gershon have since passed away.

Blanche (b. 1926) married Charles Joseph Knowles in 1948 while Jeane (b. 1927) wed Stuart Duncan Gilchrist in 1957.

Louis (b. 1931) is listed in numerous editions of "Who's Who in Technology" and of "American Men and Women of Science," the latest in 2006. A graduate of the University of Florida's School of Engineering, he is a chemical engineer, now retired, and lives near St. Louis.

Frances (d. 2002), her husband Roy Simpson (d. 1997), and their son, also named Roy, are buried at Holy Trinity.

One other Bosanquet, not directly connected to Holy Trinity, shows up in the history of the area. In September 1893, Charles Richard Bosanquet purchased a lot in Leesburg from the Stapyltons for $140. He was a cousin of Louis and was a lay reader in Montclair. On June 22, 1898, he enlisted into service in the Spanish-American War as a private with a Florida Volunteer Infantry Regiment and was mustered out about seven months later. According to the parish register at St. James, he returned to England before 1900.

Vestry minutes resume with an important decision

Following a lengthy suspension, as noted earlier, vestry minutes were again kept beginning in December 1914, just in time to record a monumental decision.

George Ward was Holy Trinity's priest then, having served for about two years. And Cameron Mann had recently become bishop for the missionary district, taking over for William Crane Gray who had retired.

The first meeting following the restarting of the minutes was held at the Leesburg State Bank – Frank Cooke, a vestry member, was the bank's president—and was marked by discussion and action on a proposal to move the church to a lot in Fruitland Park. All three vestrymen—Villiers Chernocke Smith and Louis Bosanquet as well as Cooke—voted "no" on this plan. The conclusion, according to the minutes, was that this move was "not practical." The rationale behind this proposition is not completely clear. Diocesan records show that Bishop Mann asked that the move be made. Logistics may have also been a factor as more people by that time were starting to live farther from the church. At any rate, cost was most likely a key determinant in the negative vote.

Women keep the church afloat

Whereas men were largely responsible for the founding of Holy Trinity and for maintaining it in the early years, a small number of women greatly sustained it for at least three-quarters of a century. Without the efforts of this group it is quite likely that the church would have gone under.

The women's first major contribution was the organization of the Holy Trinity Guild on Jan. 22, 1915, only about a month after the resumption of the vestry minutes, with Carrie Wightman as president. Annie West succeeded her in 1923.

According to Dorothy Paddock, the formation of the guild "marked a new chapter of solid growth, extending the work and mission of the church further among the women and into the community."

The little group of nine or ten met weekly and initially devoted its efforts to sewing aprons and making other items for bazaars as well as planning suppers to benefit Holy Trinity.

In 1916, in order to better assist in World War I work in the area, it suspended its activities and merged temporarily with women from other community churches to create the "Fruitland Park Patriotic Association." Regular weekly guild meetings didn't resume until January 1919.

The Women of the Guild on dedication day

Once the guild reactivated, it concentrated over the next few years on obtaining a meeting place of its own. Paddock explained, "A lot was donated in 1920 by a Dr. MacKenzie of the Land Company on Berckman St. [at the corner with Park] and this lot was traded in the following year by the canny ladies for a cottage next door, the 'Boyer Place', for the additional price of 27 aprons!" (Another probably more accurate but less interesting record gives the total cost of the building as $300.) Although this house was locally notorious as the site of a still, with marks of barrels permanently indented in the floor, the guild members went to work immediately, making it, said Paddock, "sightly without and suitable within." On April 6, 1922, the guild hall was dedicated, becoming a home for the women of Holy Trinity Church for nearly forty years.

The facility also served as a regular weekly meeting place for the church's Sunday School since it was more convenient to where many of the children lived. Annual meetings of the church and mid-week Lenten services were also held there.

Summarized Paddock, "In addition to the social and spiritual benefits of working together, the women were making a real material contribution to the needs of the church."

During Wilson's watch . . .

In 1921 Rev. Ward resigned and was replaced by Francis J. Wilson. At the time Ward departed, he was paid $16 per Sunday. There were 35 confirmed adult members at Holy Trinity, and the church had a reported annual income of just over $600. Finances would improve slightly under Wilson; he also introduced the offering envelopes and a parish budget.

The vestry still held many meetings at the rectory in Leesburg, and Holy Trinity shared a number of expenses with St. James, as in the past. However, membership would remain about the same. The total value of church properties was set at $12,000 when Wilson left.

George Winter, Alfred Bosanquet and Ormond Vickers-Smith were elected to the vestry in 1922.

Easter Day 1923

There were generally just two services a month at that time—Evening Prayer every other Sunday afternoon, occasionally followed by teas at Bosanquets'.

Shortly after Wilson came on board, the Missionary Diocese of South Florida was disbanded and the Diocese of South Florida was formed. Cameron Mann had had as one of his goals the achievement of independent diocesan status for South Florida, and he continued as bishop in the newly created entity.

In April 1924 J.M. Palmer was authorized to change the church doors to open outward. The vestry minutes note this change as "a great improvement to the church." A few months previously he had

The Rev. Francis J. Wilson

been asked to make shelves—located by the south door and still in use today—for prayer books and hymnals.

Villiers Chernocke Smith

Villiers Chernocke Smith was a well-known early citrus grower, a founder and the oldest member of the church. Senior warden from 1892 to 1924, he was in a train accident and left for England to recover. He died there shortly thereafter. "The Good Shepherd" stained glass window above the altar was given in his memory in 1926. This window replaced one called "The Bleeding Heart of Jesus" that was reportedly thought to be too Catholic. What happened to the original is unknown.

Prior to the installation of the new stained glass, the vestry agreed to have a morning service on the fifth Sunday of any month that had one. And in March 1925 the church tower was taken down because of "it being unsafe and always leaking. Re-roof with the 'best grade cypress shingles.' " (Bats were also a problem, and the new shingled roof eventually leaked as well.)

The Good Shepherd
Window

The Southern Glass Co. in Jacksonville submitted the design for the new window for $500. At first, according to its minutes, "The Vestry viewed the Memorial East Window in St. James Church, Leesburg, the subject being that of the Good Shepherd, and the general impression seemed to be that they did not favor the two windows being too much alike. However, two months later, the group met with a representative of the glass company who presented other designs. A decision was then made to go with the original design with 'two side windows in a conventional design in tinted glass' for a total cost of $550."

Additional pews, copies of the originals made by Jonathan Luther in the 1890s, were installed during the 1920s to bring seating in the church to its present capacity.

On a different note, Holy Trinity member Lillian Dyer Vickers-Smith's "History of Fruitland Park" was first published in 1924 and re-issued in 1926. In 1929 she co-authored "The History of Lake County, Florida" with Umatilla's William T. Kennedy, long-time county superintendent of education. Both publications have been very helpful as resources in the writing of this book.

A woman who "fell" into journalism, Lillian did her first news writing for the Fruitland Park Chamber of Commerce and eventually worked for several newspapers, one being the Orlando Sentinel.

"At the height of her career in journalism, she became a sports editor, possibly the first female one in history, I think," said Ormund Powers in an article about her that appeared in the Sentinel on May 15, 1996. "She was not only tireless, she was good. She worked so hard at covering sports events, particularly baseball, that the old Florida State League made her its official scorekeeper."

Born in Rutland, Vt, she came to Lake County in 1919 following her marriage to Ormond Vickers-Smith. Ormond was a contractor, World War I veteran, vestryman (as noted earlier) and Fruitland Park native, and both he and she came from distinguished ancestry in England.

The Blackford era

The Rev. Randolph Fairfax Blackford

Just before the Great Depression hit the country, St. James in Leesburg became a parish and called Randolph Fairfax Blackford as its rector. Because Holy Trinity remained a mission and was yoked with St. James, Blackford, who succeeded Francis Wilson, was designated priest-in-charge here. He served through the Depression and beyond before leaving the area in 1939. Along with his wife, Ellen, he is buried in the churchyard.

Holy Trinity was fortunate to escape any major setbacks during this period, although the balance in the general fund dipped to 41 cents in September 1933. Blackford made a noble gesture by voluntarily reducing his stipend to help meet expenses. According to Dorothy Paddock, "His most notable quality was his generosity, which made it nearly impossible to present him with any sort of monetary or material gifts, since these always ended up in the pocket of someone he considered more needy than he."

Several significant changes occurred during Blackford's tenure which started in mid-December 1928.

To begin with, he immediately included an extra Sunday service. Along with continuing Evening Prayer at 3 p.m. on the first and third Sundays, he added Holy Communion on the second one at 8 a.m. He also celebrated Holy Communion on Christmas Day at 10 a.m.

In 1932, John D. Wing took over from Cameron Mann as Bishop of the Diocese of South Florida. Wing was an advocate of racial equality. Under his leadership, the diocese not only survived but began to thrive.

Two years later an altar guild was organized among the younger women to maintain the vestments, altar cloths, brassware and other furnishings used at services. The preservation of many of the original embroideries is also due to the efforts of this group. Ruth Bosanquet may have actually gotten this guild started while Isabelle "Babe" Ruser served as director for over 30 years. Mildred Clark, Eleanor Frame, Geneva Kramer, Lucy LaBorde, Betina Morrow, Frances Newell and Lillian Vickers-Smith were among the other initial members.

A record number of 150 worshiped at the Easter service of 1935. This figure would not be surpassed for about another 15 years.

The fiftieth anniversary of the church was celebrated in February 1936 with a 3 p.m. Evening Prayer service, followed by a "high tea" at Bosanquets' and then a special commemorative ceremony at 5 p.m. One hundred fifteen people were in attendance for this celebration. Secretary-treasurer Walter Clark gave a favorable financial report and junior warden Ormond Vickers-Smith read letters of congratulations from several former priests.

Soon thereafter, a decision was made to set aside the third Sunday in February each year as Founders' Day. According to vestry minutes, "This anniversary falls in June but the majority of communicants have returned North by that time, and it was felt advisable to have the day observed in February." Although the intentions of the vote have never been really followed, the founding has since been celebrated, off and on, on Trinity Sunday.

Holy Trinity Mission

Following the 1936 passing of Sarah Brewster Julian, widow of Holy Trinity's first priest, Blackford was presented with her husband's communion set. It is now on display in the parish hall.

Various repairs and upgrades to the church took place during the last few years of Blackford's tenure. Among these were the installation of oil heaters, thanks to the women's guild. Vestry members were each assigned times during the months of November through March to care for them.

Blackford resigned March 1, 1939. The offering from the previous Sunday, $21.11, was given to him as a departing gift.

Material on Blackford prior to his arrival locally is not readily available. Among the few things that are known is that as a young man he received an invitation to a dance at the White House; no other information could be found about this matter. Also, during World War I he served as a chaplain with the American Expeditionary Force in France.

He may have left Holy Trinity, according to a notation at the Leesburg Heritage Society, because "many criticized his progressive social programs." He was an early civil rights activist who, it was claimed, wanted to develop an African-American Episcopal Church in Leesburg. From here he went to Homestead, Fla., for several years and after that served about 13 years at Trinity Episcopal Church in Alpine, Ala.

The last local colonist passes

When R.F.E. "Frank" Cooke was last mentioned, he had arrived in the English Colony as a young man of 26 to learn about planting citrus. Among the founders of Holy Trinity (and later a vestryman), he had branched out from citrus growing to try his hand in photography for a while, then went into banking in 1890 with Granville Chetwynd-Stapylton and Hugh Budd. The latter endeavor in particular brought him fame and recognition throughout this area.

Robert Francis Edward Cooke

He died at his home of Franmar on Zephyr Lake on Sunday night, March 18, 1934, the lone remaining member of the original colony still living in Lake County. The cause was heart-related.

Word of his passing spread quickly.

The funeral was held at Holy Trinity that Tuesday afternoon with burial at Shiloh Cemetery in Fruitland Park. Later he was re-interred at Hillcrest Memorial Gardens in Leesburg. (He had been married twice, first in 1904 to Ada Gibb of London, who died in 1909, and then, in 1923, to widow Margaret Grace Cameron. Ada was already interred at Shiloh. Margaret apparently couldn't accept having him buried next to his first wife so later had him moved to Hillcrest.)

The respect people felt for Cooke was detailed in coverage in the Leesburg Commercial and subsequently reiterated in a column by current local historian Rick Reed. "As a testimonial to the esteem in which he was held, more than 50 places of business, not only stores but offices and manufacturing establishments, closed their doors at 3:30 Tuesday afternoon and remained closed and inactive until 5:00," Reed's column says in quoting the Commercial. "There were more people outside the church than could find seats inside."

The column and the story upon which it was based also cite the relationship of funeral director Bishop Dean Harris and Cooke. "When Harris was a young man, not even of age, without collateral or security, the man whose funeral he was directing loaned him the money with which he set up in business. And among the congregation at the little church were many men and women who could recount personal experiences equally as cherished. Men as well as women wept at the funeral."

Cooke had continued in the citrus business even after he went into banking.

When he hooked up with Stapylton and Budd as assistant cashier at the Leesburg and County State Bank in 1890, times were good for several years. But then, following the Great Freeze and the freeze of 1899, "So many people left the State . . . including the bank's stockholders and directors that it was impossible to carry on as an incorporated bank," according to Reed. The year after Stapylton's death in 1902, the charter was surrendered. Cooke and Budd formed a partnership, bought out the other stockholders and continued for several years under the name of Budd and Cooke, Bankers.

This partnership was dissolved in 1907, and the bank then became known as the Leesburg State Bank with Cooke as cashier. He became president in 1917 and continued in this role until, following a bank moratorium of March 4, 1933, the bank didn't reopen. Its affairs were taken over by the First National, and Cooke was made chairman of the board, a position he held at the time of his death.

In its tribute to him, the Commercial says, "Hardly a venture of note in this section did not receive his support in a financial way as well as an advisory capacity, and many of the businesses that are alive in Leesburg today owe their start to his influence plus some capital. He built many buildings in Leesburg and assisted in financing many more, and some of the most substantial buildings as well as some of the most substantial business firms owe their origin to him."

The newspaper claimed that when he lost money he personally took the risk but when everything worked the bank got the credit.

Gilbert Leach, editor of the Commercial and a good friend, wrote, "How Frank Cooke ever found time to look after the details of all other folks' troubles he assumed, nobody has ever discovered. Widows came to him with their affairs and he did his best—which was good—to help them. Men of affairs sought his advice and assistance—and got both. Minor children who constituted an estate looked upon him as a godfather, and he did not fail them."

The Dwights and Pine Eden

Although they were seasonal residents and without the large family tree or the longevity of the Bosanquets, the Dwights were also part of Fruitland Park's "high society" for an extended period.

William G. and Minnie R. Dwight were in the daily newspaper business, he as a publisher and she as an editor. William had founded the Holyoke, Mass., Transcript. As previously mentioned, they were part of the Fruitland Park "Winter Colony" trend that began in the late 1880s and they first came to the area in the winter of 1902 to visit their friends, the W.T. Deans. After spending several years as the Deans' guests, the Dwights purchased Pine Eden, located on Fountain Lake (on the west side of Rose Avenue across from Fountain Avenue).

Minnie Dwight

William Dwight

Minnie Dwight in particular had big interests in philanthropy and service to others. In Holyoke she had headed a variety of movements to create a more compassionate city. Among these were the development of the first municipal playgrounds; the Holyoke Home for Aged People, one of the first such institutions to house both sexes; and the first purely municipal milk station to be established in New England. In Fruitland Park, she entertained the senior class of Leesburg High School at a tea every spring and hosted the debutante balls, continuing these events until her death in 1957. She also donated playground equipment and other items to a local school at Christmas.

The Dwights were probably best known, however, for hosting a big garden party each spring. This tradition dated back to shortly after their arrival in Fruitland Park. As described by Dorothy Paddock, "The spacious and lovely home and gardens of the estate . . . had been, since the first decade of the century, a social and cultural center. Each spring 'the season' had culminated in a large garden party with tennis tournaments and boating regattas as well as shuffleboard and golf matches, card games, and all manner of entertainment for the winter guests who flocked to the estate." The tennis competitions were perhaps the main attractions with four cups, the most prestigious being the Pine Eden trophy, awarded to the winners.

William Dwight died suddenly just before the 1930 party, and soon thereafter Minnie made the affairs into benefits for Holy Trinity. The church relied a great deal on proceeds from fund raisers until it became a parish in the 1960s.

Paddock said, "Assisted by members of the Guild, who sewed, solicited gifts and prizes, and cooked and served a 'Sunset Supper' to hundreds of guests, this enterprise became, and remained the major Guild activity and source of funds. In addition, the increasing number attending each year from other areas of the state served as an unequaled promotional boost for so small a church in so tiny a town."

The first garden party for Holy Trinity in 1932 netted $100 and, in 1938, at the last event during Blackford's tenure, the amount reached $634. Ten years later the total had grown to $2,383, while the final activity, held a few months before Minnie Dwight's death, saw the biggest profit of $2,847.

Costs of the priest's stipend and repairs and improvements to the church buildings and properties were some of the things that the funds helped subsidize.

Among their non-church-related endeavors, the Dwights bought the casino from its builder, George T. Clark. The Dwights added a piano to the building's amenities. In 1948 Minnie donated it to the city.

William's funeral was held at Holy Trinity and he was buried in Holyoke.

His wife is also interred in Massachusetts. In 1965 a new carillon in Holyoke was dedicated to her.

Between Blackford and Covell

Five priests served Holy Trinity in the dozen or so years immediately following Randolph Blackford. The first of these was Frank E. Pulley, whose tenure was from 1939 until March 1942.

The installation of electric lighting in the church was perhaps the biggest accomplishment of the Pulley period. The lighting was a gift of Edna Walford who moved here from Brooklyn with her husband, Frank, during the 1920s. A year earlier she had donated a new organ.

Two interesting things occurred with Pulley after he left Holy Trinity. First, he was appointed by President Harry S. Truman to two terms (probably eight years total) as chaplain at the U.S. Military Academy at West Point, N.Y. Secondly, after he was in semi-retirement, he appeared on an episode of the TV show "What's My Line," stating his occupation as "raising worms." He never told the audience why he raised them; possibly he did so for fishing bait.

The Rev. Frank E. Pulley

Following Pulley, Frank Shore and James McConnell came on board until 1944 or 1945.

It needs to be noted that trying to compile an accurate account of Holy Trinity's priests and dates of service prior to its parish status is difficult. Source materials differ. This problem is further complicated since, by at least the early years of the 20th century, St. James was definitely the "mother church" in its continuing shared arrangement with Holy Trinity. During Blackford's tenure, St. James became a parish and its leadership among area Episcopal churches solidified. Beginning with Blackford and until the arrival of Fred Paddock at Holy Trinity in 1961, various other clergy besides the rector at St. James were sometimes involved but the Leesburg rector was always the priest-in-charge.

The vestry minutes from 1956 through 1960 and the service registers from 1947 through 1972 are missing. Their absence obviously hampers the assembling of an historical record.

It is known that the vestry met irregularly during the post-World War II era and many times only reviewed finances. For many years meetings were generally held at the rectory at St. James. Also, as was mentioned previously, the bishop appointed vestry members until Holy Trinity achieved parish status in the 1960s.

One amusing entry from the minutes from this period is dated April 6, 1943. It read, "Mr. McConnell was then asked to chase mosquitoes while the vestry decided to increase his stipend."

Until the 1950s the priest's salary ranged from $200 to $500 per year.

The Rev. William Martin Hargis

By World War II, many people resided farther from the church than earlier members had. This made it hard to get to services when gas rationing began; some started attending St. James.

Shortly after McConnell's resignation, William Martin Hargis became priest, serving until 1950.

Dorothy Paddock noted "In the Beauty of Holiness," "Although the official records are missing, fortunately the minutes and annual reports of the Guild, later the Episcopal Churchwomen, begin in detail in 1946 and are continuous to the present [1976], giving an accurate account of most of the activity of those years.

"In 1946 and 1947, the ladies helped with 'Red Cross, PTA, and all local drives and established a community library in the Guild Hall. During this period another tradition was inaugurated with the beginning of the Pancake Suppers, held always on Shrove Tuesday, the last day before the onset of Lent. This is again an old English and European custom, although many others have appropriated its use."

As was previously reported, a fire in the late summer of 1947 partially destroyed St. James Church. It was determined that youngsters were responsible.

According to Louis Bosanquet, "I was in the car with my father [Alfred] when we saw the fire at St. James, and we drove back to the fire house. I got out of the car and ran into the office and reported to the chief, Bunny Stevens, 'The Episcopal FIRE is on CHURCH!'"

The Holy Trinity Womens Guild 1950

Standing L-R: Caroline Lytle and her friend; Lillian Fisk; Minnie Dwight; Carrie
Colbert; Mabel Rumley; Gertrude Hughgill; Maudie Lord; Anne Bickley; Edna
Walford; Ruth Bosanquet; Maggie Mathews; Mary Wall; Brigid Ryan; Eleanor Frame;
Alice Rice; Lillian Vickers-Smith. Center L-R: Babe Ruser; Carrie Wightman; Frances
Carey; Mrs. Cotey; Juliet Eaton; Nellie Wightman; Trudy Hastings. Seated L-R: Betty
Hanson; Alma Hanson; The Rev. William Hargis; Nelde Siert; Ruth Marriman.

After this incident, St. James' congregation met jointly with Holy
Trinity's until the following Easter when renovation was finished.
During these months the women of both churches worked together
on fund-raising benefits. The "Gay 90s parade" at Fair Oaks, the
Bosanquet residence, has already been mentioned. In addition the
profits of the Pine Eden garden party in 1948 were shared, with St.
James receiving over $600.

By the end of the 1940s, according to Paddock, Holy Trinity's
congregation had grown from 40 to more than 60.

Significant capital improvements were also made during the
tenures of Hargis and his successor, Lloyd Cox. Among these were a
new roof and new red carpeting in 1948.

Holy Trinity's Altar 1947

In addition, explained Paddock, "Early in 1949 a committee of vestry members and women began work on a landscaping program for the church grounds. At this time many of the azaleas which now add so much to the spring bloom around the church were planted, in the main a contribution from the Frame, Dwight, Selfe and Bosanquet families. [These azaleas were removed in the spring of 2008.] The 'Kentucky-type fence', with white brick pillars and horizontal wooden bars, was constructed during the summer of 1949 with Mr. Hargis doing much of the work himself."

At the annual meeting in January 1950, just before his departure, Hargis emphasized the need for pledge cards instead of a reliance on funds from the garden parties and also instituted joint meetings of the vestry and the guild. Members of these groups would meet at least once a quarter and needed a very good excuse to be absent.

After Cox arrived as priest in the early 1950's, work continued. The rest of the cemetery was fenced. The guild supported, in part, repairs to the rectory at St. James and equipment for a new parish office. The first church history, a four-page publication entitled "The Story of Holy Trinity Church" and written by Lillian Vickers-Smith, was completed and put on sale at the 1951 garden party. A sprinkler system was installed in the churchyard, and a regular caretaker was employed to tend the facility.

Inside the building, R.M. McKnight constructed a mahogany altar to coordinate with the pulpit that Ormond Vickers-Smith had enclosed a few years before.

Change was in order at the diocesan level as well. Henry I. Louttit Sr. became bishop in 1951, replacing John

The Rev. Lloyd Ashley Cox

Wing. During Louttit's tenure, the church experienced a period of considerable expansion; he would be the last bishop of the Diocese of South Florida before that entity was split into three sections in the late 1960's with each part renamed.

The Rt. Rev. Henry I. Louttit Sr.

Vestry minutes of May 13, 1952, state that Holyoke College in Massachusetts received a $100 gift to honor Minnie Dwight. Two silver cruets and a ciborium (bread box) were to be purchased but there is no record of what happened as a result of this directive.

"At this point with their financial status well established and their numbers increasing," wrote Paddock, "the congregation of Holy Trinity took a 'giant step'. At a special meeting called on August 21, 1952, the Vestry and Guild voted to take whatever 'steps were necessary for this mission to become a parish'. And in accordance with the tradition that 'the women of Holy Trinity Guild have always aided the financing of this church', the Guild voted to use its savings to 'underwrite the required budget' and to sponsor a Sunday School. Although it would be nearly fifteen years before the goal of parish status would be fully achieved, the congregation of sixty-five confirmed members, actually fewer than thirty families, were on their way when they greeted Dr. Herbert Covell, a retired clergyman . . . as a voluntary supply priest at a Parish Supper" late in 1952.

Setting the table

Holy Trinity got a lot more than it might have really expected from Dr. Covell.

A veteran of the Spanish-American War and a chaplain in both World Wars, he also saw service in the French army and served seven parishes. Because of pensions, he refused a salary from Holy Trinity. He was certainly among the oldest Episcopal priests and, before he was finished, perhaps *the* eldest, serving a church.

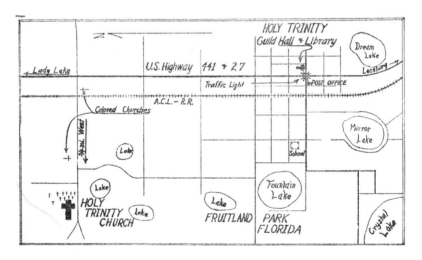

1955 map of church area

Asked to describe Covell, who arrived here at age 82, current member Betty Hastings recalled that he was thin, wore sandals (uncommon for men at the time), and flipped ash from his cigarettes.

An un-bylined article in the Orlando Sentinel of March 1, 1959, notes that he was "a small, wiry man with a perpetual twinkle in his eyes, and a knack for tumbling words out almost faster than one can grasp them."

During his tenure, the closest family lived two miles from church. Holy Trinity was the only church in the diocese not located in a town. To get to services people drove down the old clay road from ten different towns; one woman reportedly came 21 miles in a truck.

His time here began on a sad note with the death of the last remaining founder, Laura Gomperts, in 1953. A music director for over 25 years at the church and never married, she had lived in Lady Lake after she moved from Brooklyn with her parents, Charles and Amanda, sometime after 1880. Charles had been a diamond broker in New York and was listed in Florida censuses as a farmer and citrus grower.

After that things at church became more positive and a period of steady growth occurred.

"From the time of Dr. Covell's arrival until his retirement in 1960, Holy Trinity gradually became under his gentle guidance the nucleus of a true parish 'family,'" explained Dorothy Paddock. "He urged both the vestrymen and the women of the guild to locate the center of their church activity on the church property."

The New Sunday School Building

Toward this end, over a several-year period, money was raised and then construction done on a new Sunday School building. The facility was consecrated by Bishop Louttit in December 1959. It is now used for the church offices.

The 1955 Boys Choir
The Rev. Dr. Herbert Edson Covell, back row left.

A new boys chorus sang for the Christmas services in 1953. The guild funded the robes for this group, directed by Ethel Hanford.

Some things never seem to change: Paddock said that the vestry minutes of September 1956 show Covell asking that he be allowed to pay singers $1 a month to help keep up choir attendance. If a boy missed even one Sunday, he would get no money that month.

During his first few years here Covell roomed next door to the guild hall. In the summer of 1955, the hall was altered to include a room and bath for the priest. The guild also financed a carport for him.

In describing his ministry Dorothy Paddock wrote, "The elderly priest . . . was tireless in his efforts, making calls within a radius of thirty miles, concerned not only for the older members, but also involved with the children and young people in the choir, the acolytes, and church school . . .[The vestry minutes of January, 1957, she said, noted that he was traveling over 1000 miles a month to visit parishioners.] His particular mission and faith are best expressed in a quotation from the guild minutes for January, 1954; in discussing a request from the Bishop for contributions toward a fund for the work of the church world-wide, he stated 'that he felt it was necessary to develop in the people a consecrated love for Holy Trinity Church and its place in the community, and a realization of what the church might mean to them personally' before looking farther afield.'"

Under Covell's direction, the congregation grew. Vestry minutes in 1955 report a membership of 114 while stating that the seating capacity was 120.

The purchase of a new organ and the extension and fencing of the churchyard to the east were other guild-funded improvements made during this period. Minutes for May 1956, according to Paddock, said a new organ was needed before Easter, the present one being beyond repair. The women also supported the burgeoning church school. Nancy Newell was the first Sunday School superintendent.

Priscilla Newell's Sunday School Class

Following Minnie Dwight's death in October 1957, the garden party was moved to the casino or, as it was sometimes called by then, the community center. This gala would continue for a few more years before it was replaced in 1961 by an annual silver tea at the Bosanquet residence, Fair Oaks.

The silver tea service used at that event, long discontinued, is now on a top shelf in the parish hall kitchen.

Discussions began in the late 1950s on the matter of selling the guild hall. The Fruitland Park library, which had also been located there, was transferred to the town hall in 1959.

Covell resigned in March 1960 for health reasons and moved to St. Petersburg. He would live just shy of four more years. Named Vicar Emeritus after stepping down, he is buried in the churchyard.

Despite Covell's departure, "the seeds he had planted were rapidly taking root," said Paddock.

Much occurred over the next 15 months. The vestry and the guild in April 1960 talked about providing living quarters for a rector and building a parish hall on church property. The guild hall was sold early that summer and, that fall and winter, the remaining virgin timber was cleared from church land. By February 1961 a three-acre citrus grove had been planted.

Furthermore, in 1960 the congregation held a loyalty dinner. Members pledged funds for building which resulted in a new parish house by May 1961 and also in work on a new rectory. Plans for the latter had been drawn by architect John Albert Patterson, a member of the congregation, while Wes Doyle, chairman of the building committee, presided at the parish house groundbreaking.

Following Covell's resignation, supply clergy served the church. But at that 1960 dinner, those attending made a key decision: to ask the bishop to call Holy Trinity's first full-time priest.

Part 3: 1961-1981

Fred Paddock takes the helm

BECAUSE Holy Trinity was still a mission in 1961, Bishop Louttit recommended a priest for the church. That man, although not the first choice for the position, would definitely turn out to be the right person at the right time.

According to vestry minutes, W.K. Hart, the bishop's initial preference, was called in the fall of 1960. After he received no response from this priest by mid-January of 1961, Louttit endorsed Fred Paddock for the post and very likely made arrangements for Paddock to be available for an interview.

There are two interesting anecdotes regarding what happened next.

Current parishioner John Buzzell recalled the following:

"Happy [actual first name Lawrence] Casson told me that one morning [probably in the second half of January] he and Wes Doyle, another patriarch, were having coffee together. Wes said that he was going to interview a candidate for the vacant position at Holy Trinity. They discussed it for a few minutes, and Wes said to Happy, 'Why don't you come along?' Happy replied that he couldn't do that because he wasn't even a member of the church. He and his family [wife Bette, sons Russell and Larry, and daughter Bea (Elizabeth)] attended the United Methodist Church in Fruitland Park. Wes countered that that wouldn't matter so that afternoon (or sometime that day) the two of them went and interviewed Fred Paddock. Wes and Happy decided that Fred was the right one for the job, and Fred was hired. Wes was either the senior warden [he was indeed] or had been designated by the vestry to take care of the task. So he did: no search committee, no vestry meeting, just he and Happy. It turned out to be a fortunate choice."

1963 vestry
Prominent laymen during the Paddock Period.
Row 1: Ted White (organist), Fred Kramer, Wes Doyle. Row 2: Ernest Prevedel, John Kadlec, Lawrence Casson, Fr. Paddock. Row 3: Gershon Bosanquet, Norman Trampish, Robert Braun

Paddock and his wife were living in Alexandria, Va, at the time. He was about to graduate from Virginia Theological Seminary there.

Very shortly after the interview Dorothy Paddock, who was head of a local Girl Scout troop and chair of the city-wide cookie drive, heard from another scout leader that Holy Trinity was going to call her husband. That "other leader" turned out to be Phyllis Vickers-Smith. who lived with her husband, John Edward, and family in Woodbridge, Va. John Edward was the grandson of a Holy Trinity founder John Vickers-Smith.

Following his graduation from seminary, Frederick Norris Paddock was ordained to the diaconate at his home parish, also called Holy Trinity, in West Palm Beach. With Dorothy (Dotti as Fred always spelled it but Dottie, reportedly, to everyone else) and children Eleanor (Nell), Polly, Dolly and Cliff, he arrived in Fruitland Park on July 1, 1961, to assume the duties of vicar. The family moved into what Dottie called in her book "the beautiful and roomy vicarage, on the shore of little Lake Geneva, not far from where the 'temporary church' [old barn] stood in 1887."

The Rev. Frederick Norris and Dorothy Paddock

The new vicar had an interesting background. A graduate of the University of Florida School of Agriculture, he saw action as an artillery battery commander in the European Theater during World War II before retiring from the army as a major, with Bronze and Silver Stars from five campaigns and a Purple Heart. While driving a jeep in Czechoslovakia, he hit three anti-tank mines and lost a leg. That same day, his best friend, was killed in the Pacific Theater; Paddock ultimately married Dottie, the friend's widow. He then spent 15 years in the construction business in West Palm Beach and also owned and operated a gas station. At age 39, with a wife and four children, he made the courageous decision to become a priest. He was 41 when he assumed his duties at Holy Trinity.

Current member Russell Casson, Happy's son, feels that the World War II experience, which Paddock shared with Happy and Wes Doyle, might well have contributed to the favorable impression of him during the interview process.

Numerous letters in Holy Trinity's files, written after it became evident that Paddock would quite probably become vicar, reveal the considerable interest and enthusiasm he had regarding his new post, the first of his priesthood. He was essentially unfamiliar with the area prior to arrival.

Once in Fruitland Park, however, Paddock became a member of the town's Lions Club, the only service organization in the area, which gave him community exposure. Doyle and Happy Casson already belonged to this organization. Later the priest became the group's president.

In addition he joined the American Legion in Leesburg and was on the boards of the Fruitland Park Public Library and the Children's Home Society. He also later became a director of the Leesburg General Hospital and then chairman of its board of trustees.

Susy Brown, another current parishioner and former senior warden, recalled Paddock substitute teaching at Fruitland Park Elementary when a teacher was ill.

He had a reputation for visiting patients in the Leesburg Hospital, not only members of his own congregation but others as well, some of whom eventually came to Holy Trinity. According to Russ Casson, there were very few "cradle Episcopalians" in the church then. (Casson and his family, although still Methodists, started coming to Holy Trinity about a year before Paddock's arrival.)

Richard Sutherland, who attended from 1968 to 1995 and became a deacon in 1990, noted, "Fred really believed in pastoral care. He was very pro-active in this respect."

Samuel Hyslop, a member at the time, later wrote about what Paddock's concern had meant to him: "When we moved into Leesburg in 1968, my wife had a severe attack of kidney stones and had to be admitted to Leesburg General Hospital, and was listed as 'Episcopal' and did not know anyone in town. Rev. Fred Paddock, while making his usual hospital visits, noticed my wife's name and visited her and gave her much needed comfort and blessings and said he would visit again. However, my wife took a turn for the worse and had to be transferred to Orange Hospital in Orlando. Imagine our surprise when Fred Paddock walked in to give his blessings.

"I did not know at the time that Fred had lost one leg during the invasion of France, but when I realized he made a hundred-mile round trip, Fruitland Park to Orlando and back, to *give comfort to a total stranger who was not a member of his church*, I resolved we would become members of his church although we had never seen it or what Fruitland Park looked like in 1968.

"In May 1980 we were married 50 years, and after the Sunday services, Rev. Fred Paddock joined us outside the church and presented us with a . . . wood plaque with a mounted brass cross and two rings on the center of the cross and a large 50 to indicate 50 married years."

Susy Brown's father Sam, previously a Baptist, also became an active member because of Paddock. So did Sutherland.

Sutherland recalled how he came to join. He and his wife lived near Spring Lake Road, and Paddock made a practice of roaming the neighborhood to invite people to Holy Trinity. Paddock asked Sutherland, a railroad yard man in Wildwood, if he would show son Cliff the trains coming in and going out. Sutherland, who described himself at the time as "a disenchanted Baptist," agreed to the request and then decided to give Holy Trinity a try, although for a while his wife, Ann, would not accompany him. He said he was initially impressed with the quiet before the service as people meditated and prepared for worship.

His son Mark became involved in Sunday School as did Sutherland himself when lay reader Jim Hanford invited him to the adult class. After two Sundays, Hanford planned to be away and asked Sutherland to take over the class. But Hanford never returned to teach so Sutherland continued to instruct and "fell in love with Holy Trinity."

In talking about Paddock's disability, Russ Casson explained, "Although he walked with a limp, it did not slow him down . . . I do remember that he had a stool located in the pulpit on which he could sit and deliver his sermon. As the pulpit was enclosed, nobody could see him sitting on the stool."

Yet Paddock wasn't adverse to occasionally making light of his infirmity. For example, Susy Brown recalled, he and 1981 senior warden Chuck Herkal publicly joked about their wooden/artificial limbs. And Casson noted that visitors to the rectory sometimes found Paddock hopping around on one leg.

Casson remembers Paddock as a "good extemporaneous speaker" with a deep, booming voice who delivered 10-12 minute sermons which he wrote in spiral notebooks. He said the priest was very outgoing and had big hands and a firm handshake, noting "Fred was very approachable and could be called charismatic." Current parishioner Betty Hastings pointed out that he always emphasized the word "bold" as in "We are BOLD to say 'Our Father . . .'"

Also, according to reports, he sometimes would wander down the aisle during the singing of a hymn, sidle up to a friend, then try to out-sing that person!

Hastings and another present church member, Frances Justison, who was here at the time as well, described him as "very beloved, gentle, and sincere." They said he "drew everybody in," that he was more of a team player than a director, and that he was always upbeat, even tempered and appreciative. Moreover, they felt him to be a person who "brought out the best in everyone and everything."

"He was very approachable and loved us all," Brown said. Sharon Redding, the current music director who first came to Holy Trinity in 1969, noted that he was always kind, considerate, forgiving, "a planner" and "called everyone by their full name."

Justison and Hastings explained that, because of his stature with the congregation, his endorsement of a project was usually sufficient for it to be pursued: "If Fred said something was OK, it was."

They emphasized that Dottie Paddock was an ideal wife and helpmate for her husband and that she, too, was very well-liked by the congregation. Redding concurred, saying that Fred and Dottie complemented each other and that Dottie, also, was quite involved in the overall life of the church. In addition Dottie became active in the local chapter of the League of Women Voters and edited its magazine. And she was children's librarian at the Fruitland Park Library, a weekend Red Cross duty officer and, eventually, chairperson of the diocese's clergy wives' commission and editor of its newsletter.

Those interviewed generally agree that Holy Trinity was largely "low church" during Fred Paddock's tenure, despite processions that included torches and flags, the singing of responses and the habit of women, in the early years, to cover their heads. (At various times prior to then, members would have considered themselves "high church.") Paddock used both Morning and Evening Prayer, the latter because he liked it, and reportedly took liberties with the rubrics of the Book of Common Prayer. He also allowed animals to be brought into the sanctuary for the "blessing of pets," Redding said.

Sutherland pointed out that when his son Mark became ill on the day of his confirmation, Bishop William Folwell—who would succeed Louttit—and Paddock came to the Sutherland home to confirm the boy.

During this period, Holy Communion was usually celebrated one Sunday a month, interviewees recall. Morning Prayer was held the other weeks.

A local scrapbook from the later Covell-early Paddock era has a somewhat different assessment of the schedule. According to this book, Paddock held three Sunday services initially along with Morning Prayer at 8:30 a.m. Monday through Thursday, and Holy Communion at 10 a.m. on Wednesday.

Coming together

The 1960s were years of a significant growth spurt in the Fruitland Park vicinity. The area, largely agricultural, was about to become a haven for winter vacationers and retirees.

Change and improvement also began to happen at a fast clip at Holy Trinity.

The first part of the present parish house, which contained the current offices, had been built during Covell's tenure. An addition to this structure, which included the present parish hall and kitchen, was completed in late summer 1961. The Sunday School was then relocated from the original section to what is now the hall. Paddock and the first church secretary, volunteer Godfrey Mosher Luther, father of later deacon Dick Luther, moved into offices in another part of the addition.

The Parish Hall addition including a kitchen

There was a coffee hour between services at 9 and 11 a.m. A new church publication, "Trinity Tidings," was started. Somewhat of a precursor to the present newsletter, it was a four-page weekly digest of church news, what Dottie Paddock called "a fair amount of innocent gossip," and a poem on the back page, and had a circulation of nearly 400. Ethel Hanford directed a re-established junior choir whose members wore red robes and beanies, and the vicar started and directed an acolytes' guild.

There were acolytes before Paddock's arrival, but the program really blossomed under him. By 1966 there were two groups of such attendants – the Order of St. Peter and St. John and the Order of St. Vincent – for those under and over 14 years of age respectively. At that time, Russ Casson estimated, perhaps 15 or 16 kids served, including girls who would carry the torches and flags since they weren't allowed, in that era, to serve at the altar. Being an acolyte, Casson indicated, was a big deal for those involved.

1971 acolytes

Row 1: Lee Sutherland, William Akel, Andrew Braun, and Morris Bays, Acolyte Warden.. Row 2: Wayne Westfall, Jimmy Luffman, and Bob Blake. Row 3: Jon Redding, Dennis Hastings, Cliff Abbott, and Jack Redding. Row 4: Cliff Paddock, Matt Tutton, and Jack Westfall.

The ladies of the church – the Episcopal Church Women (ECW) – continued to have a big impact as shown by the second loyalty dinner they sponsored in November 1961. (ECW was essentially a new variation of the former women's guild and was, according to several current parishioners, made up of "older women." Its purpose, like that of its predecessor, was heavily tied to fund-raising, a departure from the focus of such organizations today.) The group had begun meeting for the first time that fall in the new parish house. Building committee chair Wes Doyle announced that the women, through the sale of the guild hall in 1960 and the donation of their entire treasury, had contributed $9,500 that year.

Paddock was ordained to the priesthood in mid-December 1961 in Fruitland Park. He had been a transitional deacon up to then.

Russ Casson and his parents, Happy and Bette, were among those in Paddock's first confirmation class and were confirmed by Bishop Louttit in December.

1961 confirmation class
Row 1: Ray Newell, Cathy Marriman, Polly Paddock, Karla Van Aman, Mildred White, and Douglas Braun. Row 2: Fr. Paddock, Mark White, Lawrence (Happy) Casson, Russell Casson, Bette Casson, Betty Luther, and Bishop Louttit.

Soon thereafter Holy Trinity, though still having such status itself, began developing a mission at Bushnell in Sumter County. It is believed that the bishop assigned Paddock to this undertaking. Named St. Francis, the Bushnell church, initially lacking a facility of its own, met in several locations around town. Holy Trinity lay readers— Robert Braun, Fred C.W. Kramer III, Richard Luther, C.B. "Jim" Hanford and Norman Trampish—served Bushnell three times a month while Paddock went there on the remaining Sunday to celebrate Holy Communion. This arrangement continued until the summer of 1964 when St. Francis was able to construct its own building and call its own vicar.

The pace continues

As 1962 began, Holy Trinity continued to expand.

Membership reached 150 adults and about 60 children.

During that winter, the church opened its new parish hall to the community for civil defense programs and for a first aid course.

The first mention of action at the vestry level toward making Holy Trinity a parish occurred at a meeting in January.

A young adults group was established with several couples meeting in each others' homes for discussion and fellowship.

Bette Casson, Wilda Doyle and Dottie Paddock were correspondents to the Daily Commercial. Articles appeared nearly every week in that publication covering church activities, new members and even service participants right down to the ushers and acolytes.

Sometime around this point, changes began to occur in Holy Trinity's surroundings. The church was no longer destined to be out in the middle of nowhere by itself. A subdivision, Piney Woods, was registered on Aug. 24, 1962, and new homes began to appear nearby.

In November 1962 the vestry approved a stipend of $4,800 and a travel expense of $800 for Fred Paddock.

A group of young people, the Triniteens, was organized in 1963. It was designed for high school and perhaps junior high students.

According to Susy Brown, Cliff Paddock, the vicar's son, was very popular and seemed to keep this organization alive. When he left for college it folded, she said.

In the summer of 1963 an addition was built on the parish house; it consisted of one large room which, with folding partitions, could be split into four smaller spaces for Sunday School use. These accordion partitions were eventually removed. Dottie Paddock claimed, in her book, that the expansion was necessary to accommodate the growing membership of the church which totaled 250 by fall.

Sunday School wing

She continued, "At the close of that year, a proposed budget of $18,000 was presented, with the provision that 'as of January, 1964, Holy Trinity would accept no further financial aid from the Diocese of South Florida.'"

More upgrades came about in 1964. Thanks to the ECW and some memorial funds, the church received new red carpeting. In addition, a better sprinkler system was installed in the churchyard.

That winter a fire at the vicarage was brought under control before serious damage occurred, but the heating system had to be revamped as a result.

The following year, 1965, marked a real red-letter occasion for the church. In May Holy Trinity was received into full parish status at the diocesan convention. This event, said Dottie Paddock, was "a proud moment and a culmination of the work begun by the congregation under Dr. Covell in 1953."

Silver Tea 1964
Left to right: Wilma Braun, Dorothy Paddock, Ada Belle Spencer, Alice Wirick,
Fr. Paddock, Bette Casson.

A month before, sadly, notable member Eleanor Grace Eaton Frame, passed away. Paddock characterized her as "a former educator, organist, ECW treasurer and confidante to three generations of young students, whose spiritual strength through long years of illness and disability inspired all who knew her." Frame, who taught at both the high school and college levels, is buried in the churchyard along with her husband, William Alexander Frame. According to Russ Casson, William Frame was the vice president of Leesburg-based Florida Telephone which merged with United Telephone and eventually became Sprint. The Frames arranged for the only perpetual bequest to Holy Trinity in its history. Other beneficiaries of this gift are Camp Wingmann, this diocese's summer camp and retreat center in Avon Park, Fla., and the University of the South, an Episcopal university in Sewanee, Tenn. The bequest is set up as a trust from which all three recipients each year receive quarterly payments. In the case of Holy Trinity, the vestry is permitted to use the monies at its discretion, and currently disbursements are allocated to the general (operating) fund.

At some point during this time Lenten Wednesday night services were instituted with a visiting priest at each. Shrove Tuesday pancake suppers were also held.

By 1966 the annual silver tea was combined with a bazaar. Church membership increased to 350.

Local momentum begins to buck national trend

Figures show that the high water mark in membership of the national Episcopal Church was achieved in 1966: 3.6 million compared to just over 2 million in 2009. The reasons for the drop appear to be many and are probably more in the realm of theory than hard fact. But thanks to Paddock, parishioners and probably the location of the church, things continued on an upswing at Holy Trinity for the most part for a number of years after 1966.

Several key events marked the late 1960s.

One of the most significant occurred near the end of 1966. Although Holy Trinity's 80th anniversary was a few months earlier, the real commemoration took place in December. At that time, the statue of Christ the Good Shepherd in the churchyard was dedicated to the memory of Eleanor Frame. Gershon Bosanquet, a third-generation member of the famed family, had worked on this project at his home for approximately a year; when the statue was finished it was relocated to the cemetery.

Gershon Bosanquet sculpting the statue

Known as "Go-Go" to all, Bosanquet, a former star football player at Leesburg High School, later became senior warden. His nickname, according to fellow vestryman John Buzzell, came from an uncle who couldn't pronounce "Gershon." Bosanquet had done eight sculptures before this one and was largely self-taught in the craft. He started sculpting about 1963 when helping his son Rick with a school clay project, becoming an avid reader on the subject and even refining his own clay.

Positioning the statue

Buzzell explained, "Go-Go's occupation was that of a general contractor, so he would have known something about working with cement. Even so, not many laymen would be able to duplicate his work."

The cement statue stands 6'2" and weighs 4,800 pounds.

The church women's annual silver tea was discontinued in 1967, and a May Festival replaced it. The festival, according to Dottie Paddock, was "built around an English Country Garden theme complete with a May Pole." She said the affair was very successful with annual profits for ECW approaching $3,000. An article in the Leesburg Commercial in the early 1970s states, "Attendance at the traditional event has increased steadily over past years until several hundred visitors from all parts of the area can be expected to spend all or part of the day at the historic site north of Fruitland Park."

Russ Casson recalled, "Visitors came to the church to buy crafts and homemade baked goods, and went on guided tours of the building and grounds." He added that the day included a variety of activities such as face painting, pony rides and a dunk tank. Sometimes people could also buy tickets to hit a junk car with a sledge hammer.

Christ the Good Shepherd

Interestingly, according to Sharon Redding, the May Festival was always held on a weekday. But Helen Randolf Peterman, who would later become president of ECW and be active in this organization at the diocesan level, noted the festival was the "in" place to go and that the scheduling wasn't a particular problem because not as many women worked outside the home then.

Further aiding the women's treasury, a thrift shop opened on Berckman Street in Fruitland Park in April 1968. (The history of this store has been recalled in differing ways by different sources so getting an accurate accounting of it is quite difficult.) Former ECW president Ada Belle Spencer, who Peterman believes started the shop, was the chairperson of this operation from the beginning until her death in 1972. Financial reports indicate that first-day sales brought in $80.

New trial liturgies began in 1967. They would lead to a major change later on.

In addition, involvement in local ministries increased during this period. The thrift shop provided an emergency clothing supply for the needy. A blood bank was established. And support was given to the Leesburg Day Care Center, to an area boys' ranch and to nursing homes.

Sharon Redding mentioned there was also a big altar guild at this point.

Although for the most part everything was on an upswing, some areas still needed improvement. As one example, Susy Brown recalls teaching Sunday School with no materials.

1968-9 Sunday School Staff
Row 1: Dotti Paddock, Pat Long, Marion Martin, Penny Tutton, and Marge Redding. Row 2: Lou Johnson, Irene Hanford, and Wilda Doyle. Row 3: Morris Bays, Helen Peterman, Richard Luther, Marjorie Wheeler, Jim Hanford, Mather Tutton, Sue Redding, and Richard Sutherland.

Membership remained fairly constant during this time, with annual budgets in the neighborhood of $22,000.

Several more physical improvements were made in the church including a new organ from Albert and Lillian Gubitz, gothic-style hanging light fixtures from the Robert Braun family and new seat cushions. Window air conditioners were installed in the parish house.

Redding explained that the new organ was a Gulbransen Theatre Organ which really wasn't designed to be a church instrument but was used in that capacity until it was replaced after Holy Trinity's centennial in the late 1980s.

An addition particularly noticeable to this day started in 1966. Russ Casson explained, "I assisted my father in mounting the flags that are suspended high from the side walls. I assumed they were a gift but I don't know from whom. I believe the inspiration were the flags mounted at St. Luke's Cathedral in Orlando."

Church interior with flags, c1970

Reportedly the banners were intended to soften the appearance of the high peaked roof. Only some of the ten current flags were hung that year with the rest placed in 1980.

The present display represents four of the 36 provinces of the Anglican Communion – England, Scotland, Canada and the United States – and their corresponding national flags. Diocesan, state, and U.S. flags are also included.

The vestry minutes of April 12, 1967, reveal that Holy Trinity still took a restrictive view of women in church leadership. Local delegates were given instructions to vote "no" on the seating of women at the diocesan convention.

Just prior to the end of the decade—in late 1969—the Diocese of South Florida, based in Winter Park, was split into three new dioceses which exist to this day. These entities, and the locations of their cathedrals, are as follows: Southeast Florida, Miami; Southwest Florida, Sarasota; and Central Florida, Orlando. The division was deemed necessary due to continued growth that had mushroomed beginning in the post-World War II years. According to the Diocese of Central Florida's website, "At the time the Diocese [of South Florida] applied to General Convention for division, there were 204 congregations served by about 250 priests and three bishops." Following General Convention approval, Bishop Louttit presided over the primary

The Rt. Rev. William Hopkins Folwell

conventions of each new diocese in December for the purpose of electing its bishop. The two South Florida suffragan (assistant) bishops were chosen to head the new southeast and southwest entities since they had already been living and serving in those areas. The Rev. William Hopkins Folwell, rector of All Saints in Winter Park, was selected for the Diocese of Central Florida, Holy Trinity's region. Folwell's consecration coincided with Louttit's retirement.

The 1970s bring big change

Vietnam and the civil and women's rights movements were defining occurrences nationally during the late 1960s, and these events certainly carried over into the following decade.

The Episcopal Church was not without its own substantive changes during this period.

Until 1967, the national church used the 1928 third revision of the Book of Common Prayer (BCP). Trial liturgies designed to explore a new revision were introduced that year. By the early 1970s, certainly a transition period, at least two paperback versions of the liturgies—the "Green Book" and the "Zebra Book"—were being used, and records show that classes on an "Orange Book" were held somewhat later.

In writing about reactions at Holy Trinity during those years, Dottie Paddock said, "Following the introduction of a new 'trial liturgy' . . . the rector and wardens issued supplemental material to explain some of the issues involved. On the whole, the congregation seemed responsive and cooperative, but the general uncertainty and turmoil of the era, particularly during 1971 and 1972, were reflected by a slight decrease in pledging and by the reluctance of the parish vestry to meet its full responsibility to the diocese."

Sharon Redding indicated that a number of members were more verbal about the coming changes to the Book of Common Prayer and the hymnal, while Frances Justison and Betty Hastings felt the prevailing attitude was "I really don't like it but . . ."

In 1976 a proposed revision of the BCP was produced; it was used for three years on a trial basis. In 1979 this revision – the fourth overall – was adopted at the General Convention. This adoption created controversy and dissension that continued for many years. As a result some people, including some at Holy Trinity, left the Episcopal Church or sought a parish that stuck with the 1928 book.

The 1979 version contains two rites for the Eucharist. Rite I is somewhat like the 1928 book which focused more on Word than on Sacrament whereas Rite II is contemporary or at least has contemporary language. The 1979 version shifted the focus from Morning Prayer with occasional Holy Communion to the Eucharist as the main Sunday service. Rite I maintained the Elizabethan language.

The 1979 book also incorporated elements from the early church such as the Passing of the Peace.

Holy Trinity and some other diocesan churches continued to employ the 1928 prayer book into the 1980s, stalling on buying new books and hymnals, when a decree from the House of Bishops stopped usage. The final changeover here seemed to coincide with the arrival of Paddock's successor, although there is record of a directive by Bishop Folwell in March 1980 to make the 1979 Book of Common Prayer the standard as of August 1 that year.

Ironically, there seems to be very little preference for Rite I at Holy Trinity today.

Elinor Newman

One other smaller but important local development was indicative of the evolving times nationally. In 1972 Leesburg High School teacher Elinor Newman became the first female member of the vestry and was named clerk. Richard Sutherland believes she was the first vestrywoman in the diocese.

Fred Paddock supported this and later cases of the elevation of women to leadership roles, according to Betty Hastings, Frances Justison and others.

Helen Peterman was another example of such ascension. She attended Holy Trinity sporadically beginning in 1967 and started coming regularly in the early 1970s, becoming quite close with Dottie Paddock. The two women had girls of similar ages. In addition to her work with ECW and its major fund raiser, Peterman taught preschool Sunday School and was clerk and then junior warden on the vestry. She recalled Fred Paddock telling her early on that he had a goal to "get me into being a 'real Episcopalian.'" In 1980 he told her, "Helen, I want you to be senior warden." She remembered

Helen Peterman

that there was a gasp when her name was announced but things turned out well.

Her son Alex followed her in that role in 1987 and, at about 30, was the youngest person to hold that position at Holy Trinity, at least in recent history.

Peterman explained that while she was on the vestry, its focus was membership. Holy Trinity was basically "competing" with St. James since St. Mary's in Belleview and St. George in The Villages didn't yet exist.

As was mentioned previously, a four-page history of Holy Trinity had been produced in 1951 while Lloyd Cox was vicar and sold at the annual garden party. In 1970, Dottie Paddock completed her considerably more extensive and updated version entitled "In the Beauty of Holiness; A History of Holy Trinity Episcopal Church, Fruitland Park, Florida." A second edition was published in 1976.

Parishioner Olive Thirsk was reportedly going to write a further update of the church's history but died in 1986 before her project could be brought to fruition.

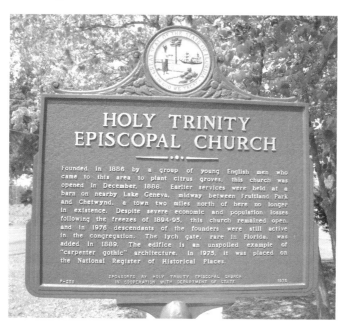

Historical sign

Perhaps taking a cue from Dottie Paddock's work, researchers from the Florida Department of Archives began in 1972 the first tentative steps toward establishment of the historical significance of Holy Trinity. (Peterman believes Wes Doyle provided the impetus.) Bruce Smathers, Secretary of State of Florida, placed the church on the National Register of Historic Places with public recognition occurring at a ceremony Sept. 30, 1975. That October an official sign was purchased.

Holy Trinity covered half the cost and the Honorable E.C. Rowell of Wildwood, former speaker of the Florida House of Representatives, paid the balance in memory of his mother-in-law, Mrs. Alice Maud Aylott.

Some of the physical changes to Holy Trinity during this period were quite pronounced.

In summer 1970, the courtyard between the church and the parish house was put in and landscaped. A rejuvenation of this area was completed as this book was being written. In addition, central air conditioning and heating were added to the rectory that year, and a sidewalk going into the churchyard was built.

Shadowbox with altar hanging

The congregation decided on a change with long-lasting implications in 1972 when it chose to preserve, in shadow boxes, the old and deteriorating altar hangings and stoles and place them on the walls of the sanctuary.

In 1974, according to the original cemetery plans, a circular paved pathway with landscaping was constructed around the Good Shepherd statue.

That winter the vestry elected to reposition the thrift shop, which Peterman explained "moved from pillar to post; here, there, and everywhere," to a permanent spot in a building near the State Highway Patrol office on US 27/441. Susy Brown thinks that by this time, if not immediately after Ada Belle Spencer's death in 1972, Betina Morrow was in charge of the shop. Brown's mother, Jeanne, worked there also. According to a couple of sources, but not Brown, the move turned out to be just a short-term solution as the shop closed its doors during 1975. Brown said the shop then relocated to the church campus and continued as a bona fide operation for a number of years thereafter.

Courtyard

As Brown remembers, the highway site was rather desolate then. She referred to the old two-or-three-room building that housed the shop as a "cracker shack."

Peterman claimed the shop "made a lot of money but was so much work." She feels it went out of business because there was no (adequate) place to store the goods although, she said, Happy Casson provided an old garage.

Another addition occurred in the spring of 1974. As described by Dottie Paddock, "One of the largest developers in the area, Bel Air Homes, offered a triangular plot of wooded land west of the church to the vestry at a reduction in price. Max Hoffman, a former assistant treasurer, and his wife, Edna, offered to donate funds for its purchase, stipulating only that the grounds be landscaped as an outdoor retreat for worship and recreation and as a tribute to Mr. Paddock." Unfortunately this plot, known as Paddock Point, has deteriorated since then possibly, in part, to the rerouting of the Spring Lake roadway.

Outreach was also taking place during this time. Dottie Paddock explained: "A supply of hospital equipment, such as wheelchairs and walkers, has been available on loan to any [within the church or community] who need them; when a disastrous hurricane struck Honduras in the fall of 1974, members of the congregation responded, with thousands of others from the diocese, sending clothing, food, donations for medicines, and even, in the case of Holy Trinity, a dump truck!" She added that donations of food for an area pantry, a practice that continues to this day, took place at Sunday services.

The mortgage was completely paid off in March 1975, marked by a mortgage burning ceremony. This indebtedness had been on the rectory, parish house, etc., and not on the church itself. Receipts from the Frame estate and the ECW helped make this event possible.

By the end of 1975, the total number of baptized persons had reached 500 and the budget had climbed to $42,000.

The boom begins to wane

As the second half of the '70s began, Holy Trinity's big boom in membership, originating in the 1950s, began to fade.

Sunday attendance between 1975 and 1980 averaged 140 to 160 with some decline in the summer. There were three services each Sunday during the time when the snowbirds were here.

Changes in how membership was determined might account for part of the reason for the leveling off then and thereafter. A posting to the House of Bishops/Deputies' listserv on Oct. 28, 2010, alluded to this matter. The entry stated, in part, "I'd also love to hear advice on how to look backwards into the books across periods when different practices may have been in force. For example, when I came to my parish 20 years ago, we apparently took people off the rolls only when they requested a transfer or we knew they had died. This left hundreds of names of people who had not been seen in years or decades and had subsequently moved without formally transferring membership or had passed away. After we did massive updates of our records, it looked on paper as though we had lost half of our membership. It's still in living memory, so we know why the numbers changed then, but it makes it hard to compare. And no one knows how bodies were counted here in 1960 or 1940. (For example, when records say there were 300 in the church school in 1960, does that mean that 300 actually participated, or that they counted every child in the parish as a member of the church school, regardless of whether they ever attended? Anecdotal testimony varies.)"

Fred Paddock continued to be very dedicated to his ministry during these years. Service registers show that he was particularly attentive to communing shut-ins during Holy Week and the period before Christmas, and also that he went monthly to the state prison in Starke to give the Sacrament to an inmate on death row.

That man, a church member and a former classmate of Paddock's daughter Polly, was convicted of murder. Polly cited her father's concern for him as an example of how the priest "never gave up on anybody." Fred Paddock sat with him at his trial and, in addition to bringing him Communion, sent him long letters.

Polly wrote, "I once asked Daddy if he thought (the inmate) was guilty. 'No,' Daddy said. 'But it doesn't matter. Either way he needs me.'"

Reportedly a number of parishioners did not support these visits but continued to hold the priest in high esteem.

Vocal music was a weak point of the Paddock period that most likely was not his fault. Although Holy Trinity always had an organist and sang hymns, there was no choir during much of his tenure, including at the time of his departure.

A Sunday procession with a choir!

Vestry minutes for the late '70s are somewhat sketchy and, with Dottie Paddock's history ending in 1975, source material for this period is scanty.

The early spring wasp problem in the church, which continues to this day, was noted in the vestry minutes of Feb. 1, 1976. This issue probably predates that time by a number of years.

Holy Trinity celebrated its 90th anniversary in 1976. Records indicate the church was freshly painted for the occasion. Bishop Louttit attended, 17 former senior wardens marched in the procession, and former ECW presidents and altar guild members were also recognized. In addition, representatives of the city, civic clubs, scouts, volunteer firemen and other churches were present.

The 1976 vestry was unique in that it was comprised entirely of past senior wardens including Bob Braun, Bill Martin, Bob Morrow, Gene Duszik, Larry Meahl and Bill Fowler.

The only significant physical improvements noted then were the ordering of air conditioners for the parish hall in August 1976 and the directive the following month to install handicap ramps at the church.

Paddock was criticized in certain quarters, particularly outside Holy Trinity, for being too tight with money when it came to building upkeep. But many locally did not hold this view. Helen Peterman thinks that the rector spent from his own resources because he wanted the church to be "just right." And Richard Sutherland believes that Paddock, as a former builder and woodworker, "would either make needed repairs himself or hire someone who would do the job cheaply."

Women continued to play a major role in the welfare of Holy Trinity. In 1977 the ECW purchased candles, wafers, wine and occasionally flowers along with place mats, napkins, paper cups, towels and coffee for the kitchen. In addition the group bought two dishwashers, a water heater and parish hall drapes and donated $500 to the parish house building fund. Furthermore, it contributed to the Rector's Discretionary Fund (Paddock said they were the fund!), the Spring Lake Volunteer Fire Department, the Fruitland Park scout pack, the Lake County Boys' Ranch, Camp St. Francis (a former diocesan facility for underprivileged children who weren't Episcopalian), Camp Wingmann, and the Bishop Grey Inn (a Davenport, Fla, building, now a nursing home and no longer supported by the Diocese of Central Florida). The ECW also provided a scholarship for a school in the Diocese of Honduras.

The following year Sharon Redding became possibly the first female lay reader at Holy Trinity.

Her license for this position did not permit her to serve as a chalice bearer/Lay Eucharistic Minister (LEM). LEMing wasn't instituted until the early 1990s.

The 90th anniversary of the building itself was celebrated in June of 1979. According to an article by Norma Hendricks in the Leesburg Commercial on June 11 of that year, "The crowd was so large at the service Sunday . . . that all the people could not get inside so chairs were set on the porches and the doors opened wide so they could follow the service."

Hendricks noted an interesting and unusual matter that occurred on the porches at this event.

"A large size spotted coachdog which had accompanied its master was determined to go inside for the service," she wrote, "and skirmishes took place at the door and another to thwart entrance of the animal.

"A little fellow dressed fit to kill in light blue suit, complete with vest and tie, entered the fray and attempted to lure and then drag the dalmatian away from the entrance.

"The dog set his feet, and young Mike Casson [son of Larry and Elaine Casson] hung on to his collar and managed to skid him a little way before the dog knocked Mike flat on his back, somewhat to the detriment of Mike's shining clean attire.

"Samuel Hyslop bribed Mike to cease and desist his efforts, with a piece of candy magically produced from a pocket, as the dog was showing a healthy set of teeth.

"And as quiet was temporarily restored to the patio, five doves, flying in perfect formation, came wheeling in over the church."

During 1979 workers restored parts of Holy Trinity that had been extremely damaged by termites.

Thom Weekley—a lay reader, vestry member and middle school teacher—decided to create commemorative gifts for all parishioners who donated to the restoration. (The balance of the funding came from a matching state grant.) Weekley was inspired months before by a Lenten service movie entitled "On Coventry Cathedral." The film recounted a 1940 air raid which reduced an English church to ruins. There, someone shaped three remaining nails from the building into a cross which became a symbol of the cathedral's Ministry of International Reconciliation. Weekley used portions of the nails left when the damaged original wood from Holy Trinity was burned to fashion 114 crosses given to the donors at the Epiphany service Jan. 6, 1980. The only differences between his crosses and those at Coventry were that Weekley's were made from smaller nails and were painted black.

Holy Trinity served as a meeting place for various community groups at this time including two scout troops, the Spring Lake Volunteer Fire Department and a local branch of Alcoholics Anonymous. In addition, the rector's discretionary fund and food closet, which was maintained in the kitchen, served about 150 people seeking emergency help, and a blood bank for members was provided.

About 450 copies of "Tidings" were being regularly mailed at this point.

An excerpt from an area guidebook first published in 1981 mentions a change that, although unfortunate, might have been expected by this time. In the section "52 Offbeat Excursions In and Around Orlando," Edward Hayes and Betty Ann Weber's "The Florida One-Day Trip Book" notes, "For years the doors of Holy Trinity Episcopal Church were never locked. Parishioners and others could come in at any hour of the day or night whenever they needed a quiet place for meditation, supplication, or thanksgiving, but now, dismayingly, because of recent acts of vandalism, the church is mostly locked."

Paddock Point was dedicated by retired Bishop Louttit on Palm Sunday, April 12. It was intended to be a mini community park and picnic shelter.

The Rev. Deacon
Richard Mosher Luther

On Easter the following Sunday, the dedication of a memorial garden around the Good Shepherd statue took place. At that time, too, an announcement was made that the Tommy Thomson family, Dottie Paddock's relatives, were giving $1,000 to Holy Trinity and Fruitland Park to erect a small, open-air gazebo on Paddock Point. C.O. and Dot Rabon donated a replica of the church's lych gate for the project.

That spring, future revenues from the Frame bequest were designated for the building fund.

In May, Richard Mosher Luther was ordained deacon at Holy Trinity. Luther was heavily involved in youth work and had organized a lock-in in the parish hall the previous March; this event was attended by 36 kids. Several people mentioned that they remember his flat top. He later was assigned by the bishop to St. James in Leesburg.

Peterman recalls him as "a wonderful, friendly, outgoing guy." She mentioned that she and he were often in charge during the summer, including funerals. In addition, she attended diaconate classes with him for a while but then decided not to pursue this path.

In August 1980 Fred Paddock came down with walking pneumonia while on vacation. He announced his retirement, effective July 1, 1981, at the annual parish meeting in January. By March, he had been put on disability retirement. He remained at the church in reduced service so the three Sunday services were cut to two. On June 19, 1981, he and Dottie were honored at a testimonial dinner at the ACA Academy on Lake Geneva at which academy owner and Holy Trinity member Bill Horan was the toastmaster and presenter of a "This is Your Life" segment. Bishops Louttit and Folwell, respectively, gave the invocation and benediction. Paddock's final Sunday services at Holy Trinity took place two days later with the registers showing attendance of 105 and 92 respectively. Following his retirement he was named rector emeritus in November 1981.

Paddock moved to Charlotte, N.C. to be near family. He died there several years later on Nov. 22, 1986, suffering from pneumonia, failing liver and kidneys, and internal bleeding. He had visited Holy Trinity for the church's centennial celebration a few months before his death.

In 1983 he had been asked to serve the Chapel of Hope Episcopal Mission (since renamed the Chapel of Christ the King) in a poor area of Charlotte; his funeral was held there. A memorial service took place at Holy Trinity in January 1987. As reported earlier, he is buried in the Holy Trinity churchyard.

Dottie Paddock continued to be quite active at Christ the King for about 20 years after her husband's death, serving on the vestry and writing a history of that church. In 2007, to be nearer her son Cliff, she moved to High Point, N.C., where she lives to this day. She became a member of All Saints Episcopal Church in High Point and also updated its history.

Tributes to Fred Paddock

Following his death, tributes to Paddock appeared in newspapers in Leesburg and in Charlotte and also in some letters received at Holy Trinity.

The most poignant of these was a column by his daughter, staff writer Polly Paddock, in the Charlotte Observer. It was headlined "Loss of a Father" and subtitled "I feel Like a Little Girl Who Needs Her Daddy But Daddy is Gone."

In it the then-38-year-old Polly wrote, "I cannot comprehend the enormity of losing him," going on to say, "He loved me, totally, unconditionally. How can he be gone?

"For all of us – my mother . . . sisters . . . brother. . . Daddy was always there.

"And for so many others, too. Giving was as natural to Daddy as breathing."

Later in the column she explained, "In his 20 years at Holy Trinity Church . . . he never turned anyone away.

"Not the very pregnant teenager whose minister had spurned her, but who wanted a real wedding.

"Not the drunks who interrupted his dinner with rambling phone calls, or the drifters who wandered in off the highway.

"Not even the Hell's Angels who needed a member buried but couldn't find a minister willing to officiate. Daddy did. And as the funeral procession wound its way to the cemetery, his little Rambler was right up front—trailed by a line of growling Harley Davidsons."

Polly continued, "He was a tireless nurturer of those with little but their faith to sustain them," concluding, "But mostly to me, he was Daddy. The best there ever was."

Another Observer article, entitled "Living a Christian Witness," reads, in part, "As his Episcopal colleague, the Rev. Hunt Williams has noted, the Rev. Paddock just didn't know how to retire. That's what he was supposed to do when he came to Charlotte to be closer to his grandchildren. But there was need for a priest at the Chapel of Hope, a predominantly black little church in the Optimist Park neighborhood, and the Rev. Paddock accepted the challenge there in 1983.

"Church people . . . have been active in Optimist Park for some time now, and the neighborhood, once among Charlotte's bleakest, is changing. Habitat for Humanity has built houses there, and under the Rev. Paddock, the Chapel of Hope lived up to its name."

A bearded Fred Paddock

Richard Sutherland recalled that Paddock caused a ripple when neighborhood African-Americans were invited to attend Holy Trinity. He remembered a birthday party with a band and dancing that Paddock approved for Sutherland's daughter who was in middle school at the time. And at certain other functions, according to Sutherland, Paddock was noted for an "Episcopal punch" he made which was laced with bourbon.

"Fred was," said Sutherland, "the best pastor I ever experienced."

Wes and Wilda Doyle, who have since passed away also, recalled a particular incident from Paddock's early years at Holy Trinity. "Father Fred was dearly loved by all because he was *so* human," they wrote. "In the '60s, when our teenagers were criticized for long hair and beards (because some people decided it was un-American and unpatriotic), Father Fred, a known patriot, promptly let *his* hair grow longer and sported a beard."

And in an article about his death in the Leesburg Daily Commercial, reporter Norma Hendricks said, "It is hard to think of a world without Fred Paddock striding about in it somewhere, helping people with their problems."

Part 4: 1982-2009

A hard act to follow

HELEN PETERMAN said it pretty well. "It was a terrible shock when Fred Paddock left; no one could follow him."

But the reality was that someone would.

That person turned out to be William (Bill) Walters who was the curate (assistant) at St. Francis in Lake Placid, Fla., before coming to Fruitland Park. Walters explained that he was asked by Bishop Folwell to put his name on the list for rector at Holy Trinity.

The Walters family
The Rev. William and Dana Lee Walters, Rebecca and Jeremy.

He was ordained a transitional deacon in 1969 by Bishop Louttit of the Diocese of South Florida. Then with Bishop Folwell presiding, he became the first person ordained into the priesthood in the Diocese of Central Florida. "So I bridged two dioceses," he pointed out.

He had also previously held positions at churches in Lakeland, Orlando and Maitland.

Walters felt that his success at St. Francis in bringing that church from near abandonment to a thriving mission over a five-year period prompted Folwell's request for him to consider the vacancy here. For a variety of reasons, Holy Trinity had been in some decline during the waning years of Paddock's tenure and was, Walters noted, "on the brink of lapsing into mission status."

His first reaction to being on the list of prospective priests was negative. He said that he did not want to follow Paddock and was worried about being accepted. And he also wondered if he had the energy to do again what he did at Lake Placid. But when he visited Holy Trinity he was impressed with the beauty and history of the place and felt that his interview with the vestry went well.

He believes he was called in large part because he looked more youthful than his age – 39, only two years younger than Paddock had been when he came to Holy Trinity—and had two kids: Rebecca, who was going into high school, and Jeremy, a preschooler.

However, he certainly was no Paddock. Their backgrounds were very different. In addition, Walters rated himself as an introvert and Paddock as, obviously, an extrovert.

Walters was very complimentary in his overall assessment of his predecessor, saying that Paddock was "absolutely delightful" and "a fabulous pastor" and "people loved him."

But changes had been afoot in the Episcopal Church at the national and diocesan levels for several years. For one thing, as was mentioned earlier, Holy Trinity had been slow to adopt to the 1979 prayer book. One of Walters' primary jobs, he said, was to move the church into the liturgical mainstream when the local membership was accustomed to something different.

He pointed out that Paddock had some "different" ideas about liturgy. At times, he noted, Paddock celebrated from the end of the altar rather than in the center, a British evangelical practice.

Walters explained that during an interim, the supply or interim priest (which is what he claimed to actually have ended up being at Holy Trinity) was expected to not change anything the former priest had done. So when he opened the 10 a.m. bulletin on his first Sunday, Feb. 14, 1982, he said he was rather startled to find the order for Evening Prayer. He called the diocesan Canon to the Ordinary who in turn contacted the retired rector. "Oh, it's a lovely service," was reportedly Paddock's reply.

Overall Walters felt the liturgy used locally, given expectations at higher levels at the time, was too casual and needed a lot of tidying up.

Obviously there was some resistance to the change. One source for this book exclaimed, "Holy Trinity was not used to being so Episcopalian! This was a very difficult period." Another added, "Holy Trinity was very parochial!"

Walters was also aware of the need to improve attendance which had declined in recent years in general and among children and teens in particular. In addition, he said, there were a number of repairs at the church and the rectory which needed attention. The situation was not helped by a drop-off in giving by the membership in part, according to him, because Paddock had a reluctance to press for stewardship. As Richard Sutherland explained, "Fred didn't say anything about tithing or anything about giving money to the church. You gave if you wanted to give, and it sort of went that way."

Also, the choir had been largely non-existent for a number of years.

Changes are made

Walters said the task of improving the liturgy was relatively painless. First he introduced a celebration of the Eucharist preceded with Morning Prayer. This celebration then morphed into Rite 1 of the new Book of Common Prayer with some of the canticles from the 1928 book. The intent of both formats was to ensure a smooth transition to full use of the 1979 BCP. Once this was achieved, he used Rite 1 at the first Sunday service and Rite 2 at the second one.

Richard Sutherland told of assisting the priest in burning the 1928 prayer books after the church began using the 1979 books extensively.

In 1982 new hymnals were also introduced. Russ Casson recalls there wasn't as much controversy with the hymnal change as there was with the new prayer books.

Attendance began to grow to the point that the early service, according to Walters, was "comfortably full" and that the one at 10 a.m. "required chairs down both sides of the aisle."

At first, according to Sutherland, parishioners were somewhat taken aback when the priest "started talking about tithing and about needing money for this and that. They weren't used to being talked to like that." But Walters said that there was a marked increase in financial giving as parishioners "caught the vision of change and growing."

Geneva Kramer, shown left, gives wedding gift to Sharon Berry (Redding) as Genevieve McClure, Sue Redding, Betina Morrow, and Babe Ruser look on.

The sacristy was named the Geneva Kramer room in 1982 after the woman who was lay reader Fred Kramer's wife and the active altar guild director. It no longer has that name.

Closets and new cabinetry were added to this room and holes in the floor were repaired; a new roof was put on the church in 1983; the exterior was painted; the windows in the sanctuary were re-caulked and repaired; and new carpeting – green instead of the previous red – was installed.

Walters' wife, Dana Lee, has a master's degree in sacred music. She was hired as a choir director for the church while Sharon Redding continued as organist. Soon the stalls were full of singers, Walters said. The church also had a junior choir that participated in at least two diocesan festivals for such groups during his tenure. On occasion, Holy Trinity's choirs combined with their counterparts from St. James for Choral Evensong at the Leesburg church.

The priest admitted that Sunday School wasn't a strong suit for him, but this program did coast along, often with low attendance, during his years of service. There was a high school Bible study as well as an acolyte organization that participated in days at Wet 'n Wild with other such diocesan groups. On one such visit, Walters broke his wrist.

He also began a healing ministry.

The first "Faith Alive" weekend was held in early December 1982. Current parishioners and other sources recall little about this event, a second of which, with more long-term effects, occurred about 20 years later.

In August 1983 Walters introduced the Cursillo movement to Holy Trinity. This proved to be very significant to various members of the congregation. One of those benefiting was Sutherland who claimed to be close to the priest and even visited him after Walters left Holy Trinity. "My life took a giant leap during the time he was here!" Sutherland exclaimed.

According to the National Episcopal Cursillo website, "Cursillo is a movement of the church. Its purpose is to help those in the church understand their individual callings to be Christian leaders. The leadership may be exercised in work situations, in the family and social life, in leisure activities, and within the church environment. Leadership, in Cursillo, does not mean power over others, but influence on others." The site also states, "Many people have said Cursillo provides an important learning experience which causes many to feel like newly made Christians with a purpose and with support." Training is accomplished during a three-day weekend and regular follow-ups are held. According to Sutherland, perhaps 20 couples, including him and his wife, participated in the initial Cursillo weekend for Holy Trinity and were active in the movement thereafter. He said for him it was a "life-changing experience;" he loved the renewal music and sang in the choir until hearing issues became a problem. However, he also noted that while Cursillo has become much bigger at some other churches, it didn't seem to perpetuate itself at Holy Trinity as future involvement by other parishioners declined and to this day is slight.

Despite his achievements, Walters always remained cognizant that he had followed such a beloved priest as Paddock. He recalled that he particularly felt challenged with older members who had very high regard for his predecessor. "How can I be these people's pastor?" he asked himself a month after accepting the role. But he said that he never wanted to assume Paddock's mantle or for people to think that he had.

Paddock himself had apparently come to realize the difficulty he had created. According to Sutherland, Paddock said to him, "I think I may have stayed here too long and made it hard on the next priest."

Other happenings during the Walters years

By the time Walters came on board, regular church activities at Fair Oaks had pretty well ceased. Go-Go, his wife, Janis, and their children, Victoria and Rick, remained quite active, but the only other Bosanquet with whom the priest recalled being involved was Alfred ("Mr. Bosanquet") who by then was an invalid. Walters remembered that Alfred had an African-American caregiver. This employee would drive him to Holy Trinity in a golf cart so that "Mr. Bosanquet" could see it. As the patriarch of the family, Walters claimed, Alfred took the church quite seriously. He passed away on May 3, 1982.

A memorial gift of $425 for a silver communion kit was given in Alfred's name shortly thereafter. This service is now in a display case in the parish hall.

According to vestry minutes in April 1984, the orange grove on church property that had been started early in the Paddock era as a source of supplemental funding was "not only severely damaged by the freeze but has deteriorated badly" and would take three to five years to regenerate. The vestry therefore decided the dead trees would be removed and burned. But the last remnants didn't vanish until after another freeze a few years later.

Walters said that a church member whose name he couldn't recall (it was Ernie Prevedel) had groves of his own and had cared for the property and that it was a "beautiful sight."

In the several years prior to the 1984 freeze, the grove had produced revenue. The vestry minutes for May 1983 indicate that 900 boxes had been sold at $6 a box for a total of $5,800. (It is not known why there is a discrepancy in the gross amount.) After expenses, the church made a profit of $2,400.

In early 1985, after most of the dead orange trees were removed, Sutherland planted pecan trees along the west border of the former grove. This work may have been done on Rogation Sunday, the observation of which was reportedly once a tradition at Holy Trinity. Rogation Sunday is the sixth Sunday after Easter and is an occasion to recognize people's dependence on the land for food and to celebrate God's hands in sprouting seeds, growing plants and creating bountiful harvests.

At that time, and continuing for about ten years thereafter, Sutherland operated a small firm which had a contract to provide maintenance for the rectory, grounds and cemetery at Holy Trinity.

Although the vestry minutes in August 1984 refer to maintenance, vandalism, and unauthorized use issues at Paddock Point, Walters recalls otherwise. He said the park at first was an open landscape with a large sign reading "Paddock Point." According to what he was told, "Fred was embarrassed upon seeing it [the sign] and insisted that it be removed." Then the church installed a lych gate-replica gazebo. Walters remembers no vandalism and said the park was well used by kids.

The priest felt that Holy Trinity always seemed to struggle with how to economically care for its property. He mentioned that there were three maintenance "regimes:" first a sexton, then just a mower who kept burning out machines and finally a service composed mostly of mentally handicapped individuals. When that service went defunct, Sutherland took over.

Overall, Walters said, he had difficulty seeing himself in a long-term relationship with Holy Trinity. He thought he had accomplished his basic goals of improving the liturgy and the music, increasing youth participation and getting the buildings repaired. In his opinion, his involvement with Cursillo and the renewal movement changed everything. He added that experience to his resume which then caught the attention of the parish at Christ Episcopal Church in Lancaster, S.C. Following a final service on June 16, 1985, he left Fruitland Park to go to that church where he served as priest for 20 years (about the length of Paddock's tenure at Holy Trinity) until his retirement. Reportedly 60% of that parish became involved in Cursillo. He still lives in Lancaster and attends Christ Church to this day.

New "director;" similar direction

Considering that Walters, by his own admission, didn't really connect with a number of parishioners, Holy Trinity's next priest was, perhaps surprisingly to some, more similar to him than to Fred Paddock.

The Rev. Ernest (Ernie) Percival Davis III was 34 when he came to Fruitland Park, five years younger than Walters was when he started. According to Richard Sutherland, senior warden at the time, Davis was also tall, thin, bearded and introverted like Walters. Sutherland considered the new priest to be "cerebral" while others ascribed the word "energetic." Furthermore, Davis and his wife, Valerie, had young children as Walters did. Daughter Margaret was born shortly after he began serving Holy Trinity. Then came two sons – Ernest, nicknamed "Chet" after Chetwynd, and Ian Michael.

The Davis family
The Rev. William Percival and Valerie Davis, and children, Chet, Ian, and Margaret.

He celebrated his first services Dec. 22, 1985.

In describing his predecessor Davis said that, as he understood it, Walters was exactly what Holy Trinity had asked for – "a preacher and a teacher who could bring the parish into a spiritual renewal and a commitment to evangelism."

The new rector remarked that "the things that had saved the parish for a long time, we could tell, were not working as well as they used to."

However, he said, "Anyone who follows a very long-term, popular priest becomes kind of a sacrificial lamb." Walters "was beloved by a few, especially those who really resonated to his evangelical background and to his wife's gifts in music and liturgy, but at the same time he was not Fred Paddock."

Davis also pointed out Walters' charismatic ministry. "Bill was much more of a charismatic person than I was," he said. But Parker Bauer who began attending Holy Trinity in 1987 with his family and became close to the Davises, noted that the priest's wife, Valerie, was a charismatic. "People in the parish were divided about whether that [the charismatic movement] was legitimate and good," Davis pointed out. One person recalled that some parishioners responded to the combination of Walters' charismatic leanings and the new prayer book by feeling, "We got slammed!"

Davis grew up in the Jacksonville area and worked in health services in St. Petersburg before going to General Seminary in New York. He was ordained in Providence, R.I., and was a curate at Our Savior Episcopal Church in Mandarin, Fla. (near Jacksonville) right before coming to Holy Trinity.

When asked why he took this job, he said, "You needed somebody and I was available." He added, "The church had been through a hard time in some ways."

Davis noted that, like Walters, he was involved with Cursillo and was interested in church renewal, evangelism and liturgy.

Mimi Beliveau's Sunday School Class.

It was Davis who was responsible for the Bauers' decision to attend Holy Trinity. They explained that they came from Grace Episcopal in Ocala at a time of a change in clergy there. On the first Sunday they decided to attend a service at Holy Trinity, they arrived late and were about to leave when Davis, with his vestments flying, came running down from the entryway, greeted them and asked them to come in and look at the church. They said that when they saw the inside they were hooked. Said Charlotte Bauer, "It's conceivable that we might not have come back if Ernie hadn't done what he did."

As was hoped when he was hired, Davis decided immediately to put an emphasis on Christian education (Sunday School, vacation Bible school) mostly with those below high school age since, according to him, there weren't many high schoolers in the church at that time. His goal, he said, was to attract young families to help grow the parish.

The church added a new educational building to its grounds in the fall of 1988. Go-Go Bosanquet was in charge of the assembly of this prefab which was used initially as a Sunday School building, then a thrift shop and eventually as Holy Trinity Episcopal School.

Sunday School Building and Good Shepherd statue

Service registers show that for a while, beginning in the fall of 1987, Davis kept to the liturgical calendar by holding Morning Prayer at 6:45 a.m. every day except Saturday although attendance was frequently quite sparse. "I don't know if very often, or ever, people came and joined me," he remembered, but explained that "a number of parishes (then) were trying to establish a regular routine of Morning and Evening Prayer."

Davis also stated that he tried to create a weekday Holy Communion celebration. He made special mention of three retired priests – Ogden Ludlow, Jack (assisted by wife Shirley) Haberfield and Howard McClintock—who, along with Deacon Dick Luther, "were really a great help. They were quite a lot of support."

In addition he explained that he emphasized Holy Week services, saying "these services introduced with the 1979 Book of Common Prayer had not yet taken root at Holy Trinity." He further made a point of trying to observe all other holy days on the calendar, even the lesser known ones.

"I can remember one holy day service when Ernie and I were the only ones there," remarked Parker Bauer. "I was late arriving and Ernie was already at the altar proceeding.

"He was a very spiritual guy who took religious observances very seriously."

Russ Casson recalls that Davis did not use notes or speak from the pulpit "so the pulpit was removed to accommodate the choir." The lectern, however, remained.

To some extent like Paddock before him, Davis proved to be an advocate for increased roles for women in the church. Parker Bauer mentioned one instance involving a women's retreat at Holy Trinity in the late 1980s with a female priest when there were none in the diocese at that time. She asked to celebrate a service at the church. Bauer said Davis thought about it first, then concluded it was a good idea. Thus, Bauer noted, she was the first female to celebrate the Eucharist locally.

Davis is also remembered for his writing for the church bulletin about various topics involving Holy Trinity.

In addition, Bauer pointed out, Davis was involved with some other church-related projects beyond Holy Trinity that he found of interest. As an example, Bauer said, "He had done research and found out where all the shrines to the Virgin Mary were in the Episcopal Church."

Marking 100 years

Shortly after Davis arrived, Holy Trinity began to celebrate its centennial. This observance actually stretched over about three-and-a-half years since the church itself was founded in 1886 while the building was constructed in 1888 and then consecrated in 1889.

According to an unidentified newspaper article in diocesan files, the initial celebration was held on Sunday, Feb. 16, 1986. "People from far and near filled the church and parish hall to overflowing at the Holy Eucharist services at 10 a.m. and 5:30 p.m. and the receptions which followed," the story reports. "The later service was most impressive. The procession was led by Fr. Ernest Davis, the new rector, followed by Fr. Fred Paddock, former pastor for twenty years, and the priests of the Episcopal churches in the Leesburg Deanery. At dusk, an acolyte lighted the aisle candles."

Silver alms basin

The article continues, "Among the guests was a group from England, descendants of Granville Chetwynd-Stapylton, one of the founders and the first senior warden." His two granddaughters and a great-granddaughter presented gifts to the church, namely a silver alms plate currently displayed in the parish hall, a child's baptismal foot-stool in memory of Stapylton, and a framed picture of pressed English wildflowers, given by Stapylton's granddaughter, Stella Gillette Longridge, in memory of her mother, Ella, the first child baptized in the Holy Trinity church building. Longridge's husband, Capt. Benjamin Longridge, and her daughter, Susan Frank, accompanied her. Mr. and Mrs. Baron Sewter from Broughton, England also attended. Mrs. Sewter was Bridget Chetwynd-Stapylton, daughter of Granville's son Brian and his wife, Catherine Lyne Chetwynd-Stapylton.

Baptismal stool

The new rector especially remembered his meeting with Paddock. "Fred patted me on the head and said that I was a good

guy," Davis recalled. "I think I benefited from Fred telling me that I was fine and that I would be a good person."

Davis mentioned that, over its three-and-a-half year run, the centennial also included a tea on the church grounds; a greening of the church followed by a candlelight open house at Christmas 1988 to commemorate the first service in the building; and a picnic at Fair Oaks, the Bosanquet estate, on Trinity Sunday, May 21, 1989, to mark the church's consecration. (Bishop Folwell was present on the last occasion for baptisms and also for confirmations, including those of Parker and Charlotte Bauer and Annette Freeman.) Davis elaborated, "We probably labeled almost anything we wanted to do as a centennial celebration. Centennial activities were also open to other members of the community, not just church members. Holy Trinity is not just an asset for the members of the parish. People know that and have celebrated that place and admired the beauty of it whether they happen to be members or not."

More music; more kids

As was hoped, choirs were re-established and the number of children at church increased while Walters was rector, and these improvements continued under Davis.

Also, according to Sharon Redding, right after the centennial the church launched a capital campaign to obtain funds to replace the theater organ that had been in use since the late 1960s. As a result, Holy Trinity was able to purchase, from a dealer, a pre-owned Rogers instrument containing pipes and electronics. Redding said this was a very good organ, "although it was difficult to maintain the pipes because we don't keep constant temperatures in the church. It would go out of tune during a service." It did, however, start to give out sometime in the 2000s.

For a time Davis' wife, Valerie, was in charge of the music program on an interim basis; she was succeeded by Juanita Atkinson and then Harlan Ayers. According to Davis, Atkinson, whom Parker Bauer pointed out wasn't an Episcopalian, "was in a big band kind of group. She didn't know a lot about liturgy but she knew how to play the piano and could play the organ pretty well. She would, on occasion for some of the evening things, bring in people who would jam with her, and they would put on kind of a show."

Choir with Juanita Atkinson

Bauer added, "There was a big choir at the time that she (Atkinson) was there, a big adult choir, and some of those people in that choir were not Episcopalians but they came there because they wanted to be part of the choir."

Church bulletins from the Davis years indicate that, carrying over from the Walters period, there was also an active youth chorus with members of this group wearing robes. For instance, according to the bulletins, in March 1990 Charlotte Bauer directed a children's choir of eight kids. That figure reportedly grew to 18 thereafter although "18 seems high to me," Bauer recalled. Her oldest daughter, Katie, concurred with that assessment, saying that she felt that about a dozen was the maximum.

Charlotte Bauer noted that the group practiced "as soon as the kids could get there after school, like 4 o'clock."

Children's choir 1991

The Bauers' twin daughters Stephanie and Valerie were part of this choir as well and expanded on what their mother had to say.

Stephanie, Valerie and Katie Bauer

The girls recalled that virtually all the younger children in the church were in the choir. "Either Tuesday or Thursday we'd come to practice," they said, noting that the youngsters and the adult choir rehearsed separately. Then, "we (the youth) would all sing during church. We sat in the first two pews" in the choir area and "the adults were behind us."

Valerie Bauer explained, "We would usually have just one song we'd sing during the service."

The two also mentioned a bell choir which wasn't separated by age and said this group played one song every couple of weeks.

The sisters said their earliest memories of Holy Trinity began when they were five. They said they and their older sister Katie became close to Davis' three children. "We would go there (the rectory) after church," the twins remembered. "We'd go swimming, and sometimes they would have picnics down there by the lake."

Jordan the cat

Davis used a variety of tactics to bolster youth involvement, even encouraging kids to draw pictures for the covers of the church bulletins. For the centennial children prepared items for a time capsule which was buried in the courtyard area. He said, "We had some people who were very anti-Halloween so for at least a couple of years we did some Halloween alternatives." In January 1990, in connection with an Epiphany service, a big bonfire was built consisting of members' Christmas trees that Parker Bauer pointed out "really appealed to younger people." Davis also held a Sunday School contest to come up with a name for the church cat (who was actually at least the second such feline, following "Trinity.") The winning moniker was "Jordan." Bauer said older church members at first thought the cat's name stemmed from the River Jordan but then found out it was based on a member of the pop/rock music group, "New Kids on the Block."

The tradition of church cats at Holy Trinity has continued to the present with three at the time of this writing.

There were numerous attempts at youth groups during this period but assessments vary on the success rate. "The youth groups were always here and there; there was never really one that got established or that they stuck with," said Stephanie Bauer. However Katie, three years older, has a somewhat different recollection.

"That was always a very fun time," she said. "We had different activities like the Crop Walk and lock-ins."

But she also pointed out that group attendance and participation wasn't consistent. "It was a very fluid thing," she explained. "There were periods when the youth group was very successful and a big part of the church."

Comparing youth activities under Davis and under his successor, she noted that "Church was very family-oriented when Fr. Davis was there (due to a large elementary age population then) . . . (there were) picnics, camping, etc. When (subsequent priest) Meg (Ingalls) came in and the kids were older, there became a big focus on that age group doing activities on their own, separate from families."

All the Bauer girls felt that, along with belonging to the choir, being an acolyte was a big deal for kids at that time.

"Pretty much every kid that went here was an acolyte," Stephanie recalled. She and her sister felt there were perhaps 15 acolytes at most; their parents guessed closer to 20.

"I think you had to be nine (to participate)," added Valerie. For that reason, the twins' service as acolytes didn't actually begin until after Davis had moved on to another church and his successor was in place.

Unlike those of their gender during the early Paddock period, girls during this later era could serve at the altar and weren't restricted to being crucifers or carrying flags.

The twins mentioned that, like their counterparts under Walters, "Every year we'd go to Wet 'n Wild, which was a huge thing." The Wet 'n Wild trip was a diocese-wide recognition day for acolytes which, they said, began with a service at the cathedral in Orlando which would be packed for the occasion.

Parker Bauer noted that Dick Labud, who is now a deacon at St. Thomas, Eustis, was very involved with the youth and took them camping and canoeing at Juniper Springs in the Ocala National Forest. Reportedly few, if any, Holy Trinity kids attended the diocesan camp at Camp Wingmann.

1986 acolytes

A litany of other matters

For many years, perhaps beginning in the middle of the 20th century, Holy Trinity was affectionately known to many as "The Little Church in the Pines." However, over time, various considerations, particularly the elements, caused a reduction in the trees that led to that appellation. The single most dramatic loss involved what Parker Bauer said was a large loblolly pine, "the biggest one around," that stood near the lych gate and was the last tree to contain one or two of the hitching rings which the original English settlers used to tie up their horses. These rings were of obvious historical interest and were regularly shown to church visitors for as long as possible. But the big pine had been hit by lightning many times, according to Davis, and one strike apparently finished it although, as he pointed out, "We had people praying to save the tree." Once the final strike occurred, Davis wanted the tree sawed into lumber but would have had to insure the sawmill's saw blade at a high cost because of the iron in the tree; he didn't think such an outlay could be warranted.

What happened to the rings is the subject of some conjecture. Russ Casson said two of the pieces of hardware remained in the tree with one being broken and about chest high and both showing only slightly because knots had grown over them. He stated that, before the final lightning strike, the tree had reflectors on it to make it more visible to motorists at night. Richard Sutherland generally concurred but felt that a slim piece had been cut out to preserve a ring. Davis, too, agreed with the idea that the tree absorbed the devices, saying they weren't visible at all when he was at Holy Trinity but also emphasized that he didn't know where any preserved ring might be.

This pine wasn't the only tree by the lych gate to be removed during this period. Parker Bauer said olive trees that Davis had brought from the Holy Land were also cut down although it is unknown by whom, exactly when or why.

In 1986, probably somewhat before the pine tree incident, Davis, who was living in the rectory on Lake Geneva, became involved with a legal issue about a ramp and slalom course that a neighbor wanted to build on the lake for a water ski school. The church decided to fight the matter, claiming it owned land underneath the lake and thus had liability concerns, so Davis sent letters to the Florida Department of Environmental Regulation and also to Bishop Folwell. According to vestry minutes, the church maintained that the proposed additions were "detrimental to the lake, the residents, and the church" and "cause more noise which disrupts a peaceful, rural area." The minutes continue, "The slalom course is too big for the lake; is unattractive; and makes other recreational uses difficult." However, in the end the neighbor's proposal was approved. The ramp and course operated for a relatively short period of time and are no longer in existence.

Also in 1986, a group of Episcopalians living in the Belleview area sought approval to form a mission. Not long thereafter a new Episcopal church, St. Mary's, was started in that town. A few members of Holy Trinity left to join that congregation. This "flight," although quite limited, would be a precursor of things to come involving The Villages. (Distance appears to be the prominent but not sole motive in both situations.)

During the Davis years, a determination was made that the priest should face the congregation throughout the service. This allowed the celebrant to be as one with the congregation and also eliminated the tradition that God is somehow only in the East rather than among the people. Toward this end, Go-Go Bosanquet built a new altar table while re-fashioning the main altar.

The Rt. Rev. John Wadsworth Howe

Bishop Folwell retired during Davis' tenure and was replaced by the Rt. Rev. John Worthington Howe. According to the Diocese of Central Florida's website, Howe was elected bishop coadjutor (sort of a bishop-in-waiting) of the diocese on Dec. 10, 1988; was consecrated April 15, 1989; and became diocesan bishop Jan. 1, 1990. He is a native of the Northeast, was educated largely in Connecticut; attended Yale Divinity School and, in his last position before coming to Florida, served for 13 years at Truro Episcopal, a large church in Fairfax, Va, near Washington, D.C.

Perhaps hoping to further capitalize on the reputation and long-term success of the May Festival, the Episcopal Church Women staged at least two, and probably several, similar events in the fall during this period. A flier from an "Autumn Extravaganza" to be held on Saturday, Nov. 14, of an unspecified year, advertises a Christmas Corner, White Elephant Sale, Country Kitchen and a Soup 'n Sandwich Luncheon, among other things. Little else is known about these events which apparently didn't resonate as well as their spring counterparts.

As noted in the vestry minutes and the church bulletins, a variety of other things occurred from the late 1980s into the very early 1990s, including the following:

A permanent memorial for Fred Paddock, which was to be a brass plaque, was announced in January 1988.

Go-Go Bosanquet instigated the practice, no longer followed, of having parishioners put money into a little white plastic church at services as a means of giving thanks for blessings.

In June 1988 the parish held a picnic at the ACA camp on Lake Geneva with Holy Eucharist celebrated in the amphitheater. This event was likely centennial-related.

A vestry meeting in 1989 focused on "how we can become a more renewal-oriented, evangelistic church" to bring people to God in Christ by continuing Jesus' ministry through the power of the Holy Spirit in worship, teaching, fellowship and service. Three Sunday services were being held at that time – Rite 1 at 7:30 a.m., a renewal service with Rite 2 at 9 a.m. and an alternating schedule of Rite 1 and Morning Prayer at 11 a.m.

After an absence of an undetermined period, a thrift shop was started at Holy Trinity again in early 1990. Davis said that his wife, Valerie, was responsible for the reopening on the west side of the current school building which had, as previously noted, been constructed in 1988. He explained that his father-in-law had died and that, following a big sale, there were still many items left from the estate. "Rather than just hauling the stuff away to Goodwill to get rid of it, it was more of a (notion to) sell it by running a shop." Available information on the second version of the shop is minimal but it apparently struggled along for a few years before closing for good as the vestry minutes of Jan.1, 1993, note.

Minutes of 1990 note that pledges had decreased and that an every-member canvass was needed. Cited as reasons are "delicate issues in our national church; economy down," and $22,000 was borrowed from the Perpetual Care Fund. Davis was the dean of the Leesburg deanery at the time and also president of the Leesburg Food Bank. Richard Sutherland was ordained as a deacon and Deacon Dick Luther, at the bishop's directive, moved to St. James in Leesburg.

In 1991 Davis had new vestry members draw straws to determine their terms. The vestry acknowledged a $10,000 memorial from Barbara Faunt's estate. (Faunt was an influential church member and vestrywoman who was the first female accountant in Leesburg.) The plaque on the statue in the churchyard was changed to granite at Go-Go Bosanquet's expense, and the inscription was redone to read, "Come my beloved; I have prepared a place for you." Holy Trinity installed motion lights in front of the church and the parish hall to "scare off teens who were having little parties" around the buildings. An architect drew rectory renovation plans but the vestry didn't OK the work.

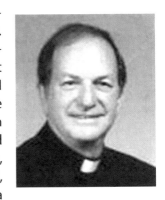

The Rev. Deacon
Richard Sutherland

A connection with Habitat for Humanity

What turned out to be a fairly long-term involvement with the international organization Habitat for Humanity got underway about a year before Davis left.

Jack and Eva Reid

John Buzzell who, with his wife, Shirley, had started attending Holy Trinity just before this time, wrote about this connection in an article entitled "A Tribute to a Carpenter" that appeared in the church bulletin March 19, 1995. The article was written as Jack Reid, Canadian-born and perhaps the early driving force for Habitat at Holy Trinity, was getting ready to move to Michigan with his wife, Eva.

Buzzell said: "In late 1990 Jack Reid and Happy Casson accompanied Fr. Davis to an organizational meeting of the Lake County Habitat for Humanity at the New Life Presbyterian Church in Fruitland Park. During that meeting various churches were asked to become covenant churches, or sponsors, of Habitat. At a subsequent vestry meeting the vestry agreed that Holy Trinity would become a covenant church. The question was then raised as to whether the church would simply donate money to Habitat or have some type of fund raising activity. Jack suggested that the church have an annual dinner with the proceeds to go to Habitat. The first dinner was held in March of 1991 and was so successful that it evolved into two dinners a year. Jack has been the guiding hand for all of these dinners . . ." [The March dinners were traditional St. Patrick's Day affairs. They attracted people throughout the area, not just Episcopalians, who were active in or wanted to help Habitat.]

Buzzell continued, "I first met Jack Reid shortly after we joined Holy Trinity. It wasn't far into our conversation that Jack mentioned his work with Habitat. The next thing I knew I was accompanying Jack to a Habitat house in Eustis where we spent the day installing insulation.

"All told, Jack has worked on 14 of the 15 houses Habitat has built in Lake County [as of the date of the article]." Buzzell added that he had worked with Reid on ten of them.

In addition to those two, Don Ackerlund, Bob Freeman, Wally Krzywicki and Milt Michaels were regular participants in Habitat projects. Richard Sutherland was also involved, in his words "mostly as a PR person to get people to volunteer to build and for the Habitat thrift store."

Davis departs

As it turned out, Davis left because of the rectory. "We would have been pleased to stay at Holy Trinity," he maintained. But, "Valerie did not like the rectory. We asked the church to let us have a housing allowance so we could buy a house. The vestry considered that reasonably but did not have an alternative use for the rectory and did not see that it would be to the church's advantage to sell it. We were in a position to make a long-term commitment there which we felt like we would be able to make if we were able to start buying a house of our own."

Vestry minutes for late 1991, the time of his departure, indicate that Davis advised the group to "let go of the rectory" and also that he left a list of things to do during the interim period.

In further explaining his move, he continued, "I had started working with a church planting group. Bishop Howe was very big into church planting and I felt that this was something I could help with so I was serving on that committee and got an invitation because of that to come out and take part in planting new churches in Independence [Missouri, which is where he went after leaving Holy Trinity and remains to this day]. I thought I was young enough to do something that would succeed or, if it didn't, I could recover from completely and I was willing to take that risk. That was a big reason I came out here. I never intended to stay out here at all."

He added, "We always consider Florida as home and come back to Florida every year."

Ironically, he not only stayed at a place he didn't expect but also left the Episcopal Church and is now an active Roman Catholic priest in Independence, a suburb of Kansas City.

An unexpected interim

Usually the interim between priests in a church's history is relatively short – and calm. Such, unfortunately, was not the case between the time Davis left and his successor arrived.

A supply priest, Floyd Adams, came just on Sundays to hold services. When he was unavailable during the week, vestry minutes relate, Ogden Ludlow was on call. Richard Sutherland, who had recently become a deacon, also assisted. Parker Bauer remembers Adams as an older and pleasant man who lived in Ormond Beach, near the Atlantic Ocean, and commuted about 80 miles one way to Fruitland Park. He reportedly received no travel expense money.

At that time, said John Buzzell, Go-Go Bosanquet was "undoubtedly the number one man at Holy Trinity." Not only was

Bosanquet a member of perhaps the church's most famed family ever and the creator of the Good Shepherd statue, he was also the current (as well as a past) senior warden and a Sunday School teacher. Buzzell noted that Bosanquet was "an all-around great church person," and Parker Bauer pointed out that the warden "never said 'Amen' because one is never finished praying." He was quite active in community affairs as well.

Gershon and Janis Bosanquet

Bosanquet's wife, Janis, had become critically ill, then passed away in 1991. Apparently suffering from depression from the loss, Bosanquet took his own life the following year. Buzzell said the church was "shattered" by the suicide, that it "was very upsetting to the entire congregation."

He continued, "We didn't have a priest at the time . . . Because of Go-Go's family background and his . . . status and rather than asking a neighboring priest, the vestry asked Bishop Howe to preside, which he did."

The funeral was held June 19, 1992, with 350 people in attendance, almost certainly the largest crowd ever to attend a function at the church.

Howe, who was in the early years of his tenure in the diocese at that point, vividly remembers that service and has spoken of the tragedy of Bosanquet's death and the sadness of his funeral on nearly every trip to Holy Trinity thereafter, according to Donna Bott. Bott started coming to the church in 2000 and has served as the bishop's chaplain several times during his annual visits.

Bosanquet and his wife are buried in the churchyard.

A first at Holy Trinity

The next priest was somewhat of a polarizing figure, perhaps even more so than Walters. This was quite likely due in part to Margaret (Meg) Ingalls' gender. She was the first female rector at Holy Trinity as well as in the whole diocese. But regardless of perception, there is no doubt that some very significant things happened during her lengthy 15-year tenure.

At the time, at least two key people were lobbying hard for the selection of a female priest while the church's search committee as a whole reportedly struggled with the idea. But in the end, following a site visit to the church Ingalls was then serving, the committee recommended to the vestry that she be offered the position.

In discussing her decision to come to Holy Trinity, she said, "I had been called to another parish and had a 24-hour window left to make that decision. That afternoon I received from Holy Trinity in the mail a . . . parish profile. I sat down and read it . . . They had just built the education building . . . I thought these are people who are working together and have an idea about where they're going . . . There were a couple other little nuggets that were buried in the profile that just kind of changed my heart." She also explained that the other church she was considering had no apparent mission.

In an article in the mid-September 1993 Central Florida Episcopalian, she is quoted as saying, "This congregation's idea of mission and my own idea dovetailed. It was a mission emphasis that brought me here."

Essentially a native Texan who met her husband, Brad, in college, Ingalls became a military wife while he was in the service in Europe. Originally a teacher, she taught at several universities after graduating from Auburn University before deciding to go into the priesthood. Following graduation from Virginia Seminary in 1988, she was an assistant and then associate at Holy Comforter in Richmond, Va, when she received the call to come to Holy Trinity. She and Brad had two children – Katie , a freshman at the University of Texas, and Sarah, in the sixth grade.

She had been told on her visit to Fruitland Park before accepting the position that she would have to spend at least two years in the rectory. Parishioner Karen House, now a deacon at Corpus Christi in Okahumpka, had been living in the building with her children during the interim following Davis' departure. Ingalls' reaction to the rectory was no better than Davis' wife had been. She and her husband kept hoping they would be able to reside elsewhere at some point, but "I never got out."

The Ingalls family
The Rev. Margaret Eileen Fowler and Brad Ingles, Sarah and Katie

"While Meg always had dreams of her own home, she made the best of the situation," assessed Donna Bott. "She was constantly painting and redecorating and managed to produce terrific dinners from a tiny galley kitchen."

Ingalls' first service was on Ash Wednesday, Feb. 24, 1993.

Everything certainly didn't go smoothly upon her arrival. Two vestry members resigned, the thrift shop closed and a circle of ECW, St. Monica's, disbanded. (This latter group had donated $1,000 for new pew cushions in 1992 on the condition the vestry would agree on its color choice of green.) A number of people, perhaps as many as a dozen, immediately left the church in apparent protest over her selection. "The word on the street was that I would only last six months and they (those who left) could come home," she said.

However, she added, "All the opposition was gone. I could start at the base, and it wasn't difficult to begin to build relationships."

During the remainder of her first year, executors of the Virginia Colson estate made the final distribution of $8,307 to the church, bringing the total of that bequest to $23,160. The piano was moved out of the church and the pulpit, which had been removed during Davis' tenure, was brought back in.

Although Ingalls was considered by a number of people to be a strong-willed person, she was perhaps equally regarded as an excellent teacher and preacher.

"Meg was a wonderful teacher—the best!" maintained Wally Krzywicki.

She also connected with youth in other ways, the Bauer twins noted.

"She had a lot of energy," Stephanie Bauer said. "We definitely liked her because she had a daughter our age. She seemed hip and cool."

Her sister, Valerie, mentioned, "I'd even tell some of the kids at school we had a female priest."

As the following sections will show, Ingalls "walked the walk" when it came to wanting Holy Trinity to have a mission emphasis. One of the projects she endorsed was the Habitat for Humanity program already discussed.

"She was a big supporter," Buzzell said.

A men's group organizes

John Tyler was one of the new priest's biggest advocates at Holy Trinity. A life-long Episcopalian, he started coming to services on an occasional basis in 1968, and he and wife Patsy were married by Fred Paddock in 1972. However, it wasn't until after Ingalls arrived that he began attending regularly. He also became very involved in church activities, eventually serving nine years on the vestry, including a year as junior warden and another year as senior warden.

In assessing Ingalls, he said, "I loved her to death but she was a very strong-willed person."

He noted, "When Meg first got here, she did everything; she wouldn't delegate anything," then added that as time went along she got more people involved as she began to see the advantages of doing so.

Tyler mentioned that he and Brad Ingalls became close despite not initially having much in common. Together with Ray Smith and Dr. John Gilmer they started a men's prayer group sometime in the first half of the 1990s. This may have been the first such men's assemblage at the church in modern times and still exists, although fairly small in size.

Tyler related one of his strongest memories of the early days of this organization: "There were just four of us and we decided we were going to put on a breakfast. So we bought probably a hundred and some odd dollars of groceries. I think we had a hundred people here with just the four of us doing everything (set-up, cooking, clean-up), and we were so exhausted that I said, 'Never again will we do this with four people.' Not only that, we lost $23."

After Smith and Gilmer left Holy Trinity for differing reasons, it became obvious that the group needed to recruit more people.

Thereafter, said Tyler, "We decided to have a breakfast every month in between the two services." He explained that by then the size of the work crew had grown so everything ran more smoothly.

"We started to make some money," he remembered. "Anytime some organization within the church needed it, we would give. It'd come around Thanksgiving or Christmas time and, if there was a need, we'd take it out of the men's group funds."

The breakfasts became more infrequent by the middle of the following decade and stopped for good at the conclusion of Ingalls' tenure. They were reportedly discontinued because the grill was found to be in noncompliance with local code and the cost to retrofit it was too high. The entire unit was removed during the most recent renovation.

Holy Trinity gets a new neighbor

For many years Holy Trinity was the only Episcopal church between Ocala and Leesburg. Then, as indicated earlier, the situation began to change in the mid-to-late 1980s with the establishment of St. Mary's in Belleview.

About half a decade later, an additional church was founded nearby in what is now the largest retirement community in Florida and perhaps the whole U.S.

What officially became The Villages in 1992 began, for all practical purposes, as a single mobile home park in the 1970s. Growth was minimal until H. Gary Morse came on board the ownership team in 1983. Morse brought a new vision which resulted in increased sales and expansion by the mid-1980s. By the 1990s, the place was well on its way to becoming what it is today.

According to Meg Ingalls, it became obvious to the deanery in the early 1990's that The Villages was really going to grow and that an increased Episcopal presence in the area was worth pursuing. She said she and Brad Lovejoy, the dean, discussed trying to find a spot of land somewhere between St. Mary's and Holy Trinity for "a nice hall for joint fellowship activities."

Lovejoy died before anything transpired and, at some point thereafter, Tony Clark, then rector of St. Mary's, began to have talks on this subject with Ingalls. She noted that these exchanges "never got anywhere."

"After that didn't pan out," she continued, "Richard Sutherland, who was our deacon at the time, and I began to have conversations about our really having to get a church . . . in between for The Villages so we began to talk about it to the region [the deanery]. Richard and Bill Furlong (of St. James) went out and found a piece of property."

Sutherland elaborated, "I was on a deanery committee. There were three of us on the committee that had an assignment to find some property up there for an Episcopal church. We went out and found ten acres that we thought was an ideal piece of property. I think it was $40,000 for ten acres. And it was just off Highway 27/441 close to where 42 crosses."

Different sources have varying interpretations of what happened next. Holy Trinity's vestry minutes for 1994 state, "Discussions begin on land in Villages offered to Catholic Church but turned down. Now offered to the Episcopal Church."

Regardless of exactly how and when things all came about, Episcopalians acquired real estate in The Villages proper. But no building was constructed right away.

What was to become Holy Trinity's new neighbor, and eventually (in January 1998) be named St. George, "grew out of a tent meeting," according to the new church's website.

"In October, 1994, more than 200 . . . Episcopalians . . . gathered in a tent (immediately south of the Spanish Springs square) to talk about establishing an Episcopal Church in The Villages," the site relates.

Among those 200, indicated Ingalls, were a number who at the time attended Holy Trinity.

"What I did was, I called everyone who lived in The Villages and belonged to Holy Trinity and asked them if they would be willing to go out and help seed this new church. We got 32 people . . . who said they would be willing to do that." She noted that among them were persons active in the vestry, choir, ECW and various church activities.

She explained that she went to all the organizational meetings so that "the people at Holy Trinity would know that it was OK for them to be a part of this."

Ingalls said that her involvement was in keeping with a pledge she had made to Bishop Howe to "do my utmost" to help get the new church going.

According to its website, St. George held its initial service on the first Sunday in Advent of 1994 in the bingo hall of the Paradise Recreation Center. Just prior to that, Ingalls commissioned those leaving Holy Trinity at a Thanksgiving Eve service.

In short order St. George achieved another milestone. In January 1996 at the diocesan convention, with nearly 90 members of the mission present, Howe announced that it had been accepted as a parish.

The website notes that, following the construction of a church on the town square of Spanish Springs, The Church on the Square

Episcopal held its first service in the building on Easter Sunday, March 30, 1997, with more than 1,100 in attendance.

The congregation continued to use this facility for nearly five years before its present edifice was completed.

St. George Episcopal Church, The Villages, FL

Ingalls summed up: "The thing that happened at Holy Trinity as a result was that we went through about five years of just grief. We lost people that were dear to us who were leaders, and our church had a hard time dealing with that reality."

Added John Tyler, "When we lost all those people to St. George, that was a big financial hit" as well.

Taking a road trip

In mid-June 1995, an eight-person delegation from Holy Trinity—adults Janet Galbreath, Brad Ingalls, Richard Sutherland and John Tyler and teens Katie Bauer, Sarah Ingalls, Amber Meahl and Michael Tyler—made a one-week trip to Honduras.

"I had in previous parishes taken youth trips," explained Meg Ingalls. "They had made a real difference in growing the youth group, and I really wanted us to get involved in missions. At the same time Don Brocaw came and talked to us about going to Honduras. [Brocaw was in charge at the diocesan level of coordinating relationships and activities between local parishes and churches in Honduras.] John Tyler [responsible for evangelism] and my husband, Brad, talked and decided that this might be a good mission to take on. We had some nice young people who were willing to go and work there. I thought it was a very healthy thing for us."

The Honduras group
Brad Ingalls, Richard Sutherland, Michael Tyler, Katie Bauer, Amber Meahl,
Janet Galbreath, and John Tyler.

John Tyler's remembrance of how the trip came about was slightly different, He said that the priest gave him a call and wanted his son, Michael, and him to commit.

Another of those "nice young people," Katie Bauer, in her very early teens at the time, recalled how she came to be involved. "It was something that was brought up in our youth group meetings and right away it sounded like something I'd be interested in. I hadn't done much traveling abroad. I thought it sounded like a very cool adventure and also a good project."

Regardless of exactly how the trip came about, Donna Bott feels that Ingalls was almost certainly the impetus. "She was very mission-oriented. When the diocese entered that sister relationship, I think it sparked Meg's interest."

After Holy Trinity decided to participate, it was assigned the mission of San Pablo Apostol in San Pedro Sula.

Bauer outlined what the group did in Honduras. "Our big everyday, week-long project was to put a floor into the church," she said. "There was a dirt floor when we arrived. We were supplied with concrete and these big brick tiles and while we were there we started up at the altar and worked our way back."

John Tyler added, "None of us were experts in doing tile or anything," noting that there were two other guys who were in charge of the operation with the Holy Trinity group "preparing the floor" and then assisting the men.

Bauer continued, "I really enjoyed that. It was fun to see that kind of progress and the results of the work we put in. I just remember that being a really good feeling."

She estimated the building to be about half to three-quarters the size of Holy Trinity.

Overall she found the church and its people to be "warm and inviting."

Tyler echoed her sentiments, saying, "They were just absolutely beautiful and so appreciative of us being there. They just couldn't have been any nicer, and they threw us a big party the last night at one of their houses. We had a nice dinner, and then they saw us off."

One of Bauer's other memorable experiences of the trip was visiting The Little Roses Orphanage. "Getting to play with their little girls . . . was a lot of fun," she noted.

In summary she said, "Being so young I experienced a lot of things for the first time in Honduras – getting to help the church, being away from my family for a while, and just seeing another culture. It was a very good experience!"

John Tyler indicated that the orphanage visit was memorable for his son as well but perhaps for a different reason. "We had four (middle school) students, three girls and Michael, going to an all-girls orphanage. I mean Michael was in heaven. He said, 'Dad, I have to go back to Honduras' . . . but never did. He loved it . . . but he was a worker."

One of John Tyler's strongest recollections was of a different nature. He explained, "When you're in a foreign country, they say, 'Don't drink the water'. Every single day, one of us (eight) went down hard [from "Montezuma's Revenge."] It was a one-day thing. You were in bed, and you just couldn't move. Everyone had their day except for my son. He didn't get it. So we called him 'Iron Mike.'

"On the way back, we got into Miami, we missed our flight connection to Orlando and we had to spend the night so they put us up in a nice hotel room. We all went out and had a good dinner. Michael got a big filet mignon. He got up the next morning and was sick as a dog. He was sick all the way back on the plane. He was 'Iron Mike' no more!"

Overall, Tyler said, he regarded the week in Honduras as "a spiritual trip."

Meg Ingalls pointed out that Holy Trinity continued to stay connected with San Pedro Apostol for several years thereafter.

Wally Krzywicki made a tabernacle for that church which, on behalf of Holy Trinity, he sent down to Honduras after the trip. [The tabernacle holds the reserve – previously consecrated – bread and wine.] Holy Trinity also paid for fans, prayer books and hymnals, and earlier contributed $800 to the cost of the floor.

Meg Ingalls noted, "After the hurricane (Mitch, which caused widespread destruction in the fall of 1998), we gathered toiletries and sent them down but at that point we lost touch with them. We were never able to re-establish contact after that. We tried for a couple of years, and then we just let it go."

Also occurring at mid-decade

In addition to the Honduras trip, a number of other events filled the calendar in 1995.

Spinning off ideas that had already proven successful at May Festivals, the ECW held a flea market sale and church tours. Bette Casson and Joan Hardesty conducted the tours for many years.

As was mentioned previously, Jack and Eva Reid were honored for their work with Habitat for Humanity.

The vestry decided to purchase a sound system with memorial funds for Go-Go Bosanquet. This system was acquired but later replaced.

Dick Labud and Janet Galbreath were ordained to the diaconate in November, while Katie Bauer became the first youth representative selected to the vestry.

The Rev. Deacon
Janet Galbreath

The Rev. Deacon Richard Labud

In discussing her position, which she said was a one-year assignment, Bauer remarked, " I enjoyed attending the meetings and hearing what was going on behind the scenes – everything from leaky roofs to landscaping to what the latest projects should be and our partnerships with other ministries. I thought it was really cool that they had a representative from a younger group and that it showed how much emphasis the church put on youth members. I remember feeling really good about that."

Although she didn't have an official vote, she emphasized that she was at least able to give input.

Michael Tyler reportedly followed her in this post before it was apparently eliminated.

Bud America became the new organist.

Meg Ingalls accepted a call as Canon to the Ordinary (an assistant to the bishop) in the Diocese of West Massachusetts but, due to the death of that bishop shortly thereafter, never actually undertook the job and asked to remain at Holy Trinity.

Before the end of the year, in perhaps a harbinger, it was noted that no one was using the nursery.

Suddenly, a school!

Not many Episcopal churches, especially smaller ones, operate schools. But beginning in the spring of 1996 Holy Trinity got into the education business.

How and why that development occurred has been interpreted and assessed in different ways. "You'll probably get about ten different versions," John Buzzell warned.

According to Meg Ingalls, "We (she and the vestry) talked (earlier) about opening some sort of school. At first we thought that maybe we would do a preschool or something like that. We had gotten the state regs to do it but we thought it was a little complicated so we kind of just let that sit on the back burner.

"In the meantime there was a school in Leesburg called Leesburg Christian Academy or LCA (which was affiliated with a church). It had been there over 20 years."

She said that due to problems at LCA at the time, "there was a flood out of that school," adding that the pastor left and a new minister came in. "He (the new man) had been there just a short time when he decided in an overnight decision to close down the academy."

Ingalls recalls that he didn't tell the staff until Friday afternoon about the closing and was planning to inform the parents on Monday morning as they brought their children to school. "Well, the staff was just completely blown away!" Ingalls exclaimed.

She pointed out that one of those staff members, Bud America, and the rest of his family – wife Karen and three children – attended Holy Trinity, and that Bud was the church's organist.

Ingalls continued, "Bud came to me that Saturday morning and told me the story and said, 'Can we move the school to Holy Trinity?' I said, 'I cannot make that decision myself; this has to be a vestry decision.'"

One of the reasons for America's request was reportedly that Holy Trinity already had a building suitable for this purpose.

Holy Trinity Episcopal School

At the time of that conversation, the vestry members were at a parishioner's home cleaning up the house and yard. Ingalls said she spoke to John Tyler, the senior warden, who in turn talked with the others on the vestry. She said the vestry agreed to meet with the academy staff that afternoon. "Within an hour's time," she noted, "we had a school moving in – and it was absolute chaos."

The staff was allowed to bring books and teaching supplies with them "but of course we had no desks," she recalled. "There were 40-some kids as I remember from K through 12, and we had to put them all over the place.

"It really changed the face of what we were doing."

Current parishioner Wally Krzywicki explained that about the only extra facilities that had to be added were a water fountain, which Happy Casson contributed, and space for athletics.

Among the various controversies was a concern as to whether the vestry had actually, or properly, acted on approval for the school. There were also claims that the congregation was never informed about the matter in advance or allowed to vote on it – although this was in truth not an issue on which the membership could vote but rather one for the vestry to decide on its own. Reportedly, the congregation's first knowledge of the situation came during Sunday services the day before the school opened.

When the school moved to Holy Trinity, it became Spring Lake Christian Academy and a small school board was created to govern it. This group consisted of the Americas, the headmistress and her daughter.

"They (the school) were very fundamentalist in outlook and using an Abeka curriculum," Ingalls remarked. (Abeka is a preschool through 12th grade curriculum employing, according to a how-to-home school website, "textbooks and teaching aids that have a Christian base. The Bible is taught through all subjects.")

The headmistress was fired the following school year. There are also differing accounts about that.

Wally Krzywicki was one who was disappointed when this lady was terminated from her position. He felt things had been going well under her leadership and that she was doing a "tremendous job." Also he appreciated her regularly meeting the kids on their arrival at school.

"We re-formed the board after that so that I was on it," Ingalls recalled. New senior warden Jean Buatti was also a member along with two others. But, according to some, that board hardly ever met.

Another problem arose during the summer of 1997 when Ingalls was attending the General Convention of the Episcopal Church in Philadelphia. She said that she received a phone call from Buatti informing her that, apparently due to some kind of spat, two staff members removed most of the supplies from the school in the middle of the night. These staffers also resigned, leaving a note for Ingalls on her desk at the church.

According to John Tyler, what was stolen were the records and the filing cabinets that contained them. Other sources, though, claim the theft was more widespread.

Ingalls said that, threatened with legal action, the two later returned the items.

"We thought that this was the end of the school," the priest said. At some point after she returned from Philadelphia, "I called the parents and told them we would not be having school – but they had (already) given into the hands of the school their money toward the following year's tuition. I said that I would see that that got returned.

"We were working on a shoestring budget."

One thing that helped was the school's access to books from the county. "We could just go down and pick up books that were really not going to be used in the (public school) classrooms, Ingalls explained. "They just gave them to us. This meant that we didn't have to depend on the Abeka curriculum.

"After this debacle (with the staffers), we had decided that the school was going to be gone. Well, some of the parents came to us and said, 'Please don't close the school. My child will never survive in the public school.'"

Faced with this support, and following a Sunday morning, Aug. 3, discussion with the congregation, the vestry determined, in what Ingalls termed a "close vote," that the school could continue to exist for the upcoming 1997-98 school year.

Just prior to the vote, as reported by the priest in the "Holy Trinity Tidings" for August 1997, "Bob Updike, in a moment of spirit-filled eloquence, asked if this vestry would be known as the vestry that could and didn't or the vestry that took a risk for the sake of what could be."

One of the provisos placed on the "yes" vote was that the school would have at least 12 students enrolled.

"You know how many kids we had on opening day?" asked Ingalls. "Twelve. I felt like this was a God thing.

"So we opened the school [reportedly on August 18] and we cut corners everywhere we could and we managed to get those kids through."

In that fall of 1997, it was determined that Spring Lake Christian Academy would become an Episcopal school and it was renamed Holy Trinity Episcopal School. Ralph Piccola was the first headmaster of HTES and also taught; Tom Boyd was the other instructor. Rosemary Piccola was her husband's teacher's aide and Elaine Pelton assisted Boyd.

An undated article from the Daily Sun that appears to be from that year states that all the students were in grades 6 through 11, that the school operated four days a week from 7:30 a.m. to 3:30 p.m. and that tuition was $2,400.

Ingalls is quoted as saying, "Holy Trinity is trying its best to be an excellent school. We want to be one of the finest in the area."

The story also reports that the facility was currently in the midst of joining the Association of Episcopal Schools.

Ingalls explained there was a period of time when "we had lots of foreign students there" as well as some who were involved in a dual enrollment program with Lake-Sumter Community College.

"We had students coming to us who were very bright and wanted to do the dual enrollment," she noted. "We did that for a few years. Then one of the things that began to happen is that we began to get more and more children who had learning difficulties. We discovered that we could get money from the state to help us educate these children and that helped the bottom line.

"As we took more of these students to help the bottom line (total enrollment was 38 in 1999), the tenor of the school changed and became more of, from my perspective, a mission of the church."

On the whole, however, small enrollment - like the 16 in 2002— has continued to be an issue, and the matter of keeping the school open has been revisited on at least one more occasion since then.

Donna Bott, the senior warden during one of these discussions, said, "We had a hard time collecting tuition and that's what nearly closed the school. We had no cash."

Tom Boyd, who had become headmaster, explained, "In the past, it was not unusual to have a family decide halfway through the school year that they weren't going to continue, and we didn't receive any funds."

At the time of this writing, Holy Trinity Episcopal School is a 6-12 facility with approximately 20 students. Almost all of them attend under McKay scholarships, which eliminates the tuition problem. These awards are designed for students with learning disabilities or special needs. But with these scholarships being state-funded and Florida, like most states, currently cutting funding in many places, the future of this program may be less than secure.

The school still stays connected to the Lake-Sumter Community College as well as to Florida Virtual School.

At least one source believes there was hope when the school began that the students would provide young people for the church and that this would be an avenue for increasing membership.

This hasn't transpired and doesn't appear likely in the future.

But that doesn't mean good things aren't happening.

Julie Sligh, a vestrywoman at the time this book was written, sent out an email to all parishioners in early October 2010. It reads in part:

"I have a good friend and colleague . . . whose daughter recently enrolled at Holy Trinity school. Almost every day this friend comes to tell me that her daughter, who has struggled in school her whole life, is as happy as she has ever been.

"Every day she comes home full of news and stories and showing off her academic achievements. Every single day she says she can't wait to go to school. And for the first time in her life she is saying she LOVES school.

"Holy Trinity school has changed this entire family's life. They have found a bright light in our school, and my friend can't find words to tell me how much she loves and appreciates our school and our church. Our school has been instrumental in changing this young girl's self image from that of a failure to that of a productive member of society with a future full of hope. What a priceless gift!"

First Promise hits home

Perhaps mirroring society in general and beginning possibly as far back as the early 1960s, The Episcopal Church (TEC) began to show indications in various ways of a somewhat more liberal bent.

As this shift became evident, in nearly every diocese a number of groups formed whose goal was to maintain, or return to, a more orthodox, fundamental approach.

The Rev. John W. Howe, later to become bishop of the Diocese of Central Florida, was one of the individuals quite active in several of those organizations.

Until just after the mid-1990s, all of this had little direct bearing on Holy Trinity. But that began to change with the introduction of "The First Promise" in 1997. This document, according to research done by Donna Bott, stemmed from a meeting of 26 clergy in South Carolina that September. Quoting from her findings, "The First Promise refers to a statement in the BCP (Book of Common Prayer) services for ordination of priests and deacons whose 'first promise' is 'to be loyal to the doctrine, discipline, and worship of Christ as this Church has received them'. The document, 'The First Promise,' states that many of the leaders of the Episcopal Church have abandoned 'the faith once delivered to the saints.' The document also specifies that there were three actions of the 1997 General Convention (the one in Philadelphia that Meg Ingalls had just attended) which demonstrate this alleged defection from the faith: the election of a primate [Presiding Bishop Frank Griswold] who has departed from the teaching of the apostles; the mandatory and coercive enforcement of the ordination of women; and the failure to uphold and require a biblical sexual ethic for the Episcopal Church's clergy and people."

At some time in late 1997, Ingalls attended what she generally termed a (diocesan) "clergy conference." She maintained that from the time of her arrival at Holy Trinity as the first female priest in the diocese to the time of that conference, she was generally ignored at such events by her male counterparts. However, as she explained, that situation was about to change. First Promise was introduced to those attending the clergy gathering. They were informed that Bishop Howe had endorsed this document and they were asked to sign it. Ingalls read the document that night. "At the point that I read that, I realized we were in deep trouble!" she exclaimed.

She said that the following day when everyone was again asked to sign the pledge, she stood up, expressed her opinion about the document and refused to sign it, adding that this was the first time she had ever been very vocal or assertive at such an event.

"It was really interesting," she noted. "The room kind of erupted." She said that another person immediately followed suit. "At that point I suddenly made friends in the diocese, and these are friends that stood me well during most of my tenure there."

When this matter was brought before the vestry at Holy Trinity, this group also refused to endorse the document. "We remain faithful to the Episcopal Church and its doctrine and discipline and worship," the vestry said in a prepared statement. "We also remain obedient to the will of our bishop as long as it does not violate our conscience or our faith, lead us into apostasy, or take us into schism."

No one really knew for sure what would happen as a result of the First Promise or what repercussions might result for churches who refused to get on board with it, but there was plenty of conjecture. Some churches, including Holy Trinity, expressed disapproval by withholding portions of money allocated to the diocese from member pledges.

Although things elsewhere kept evolving the next several years as a result of the First Promise and its aftermath, not much more happened at Holy Trinity until after Gene Robinson's consecration as Bishop of New Hampshire in 2003.

As the first openly gay bishop in The Episcopal Church, Robinson's high-profile election and ordination led to many conservative congregations breaking from the national church and joining Anglican break-away factions. Other churches that maintained affiliation with TEC, including Holy Trinity, lost a few members over that and similar matters.

In 2004 Holy Trinity's vestry again affirmed its position. The organization's minutes for that year contain the notation, "Resolved not to be affiliated with the Network of Anglican Communion Dioceses and Parishes."

Bishop Howe, despite being theologically conservative, has also been a consistent proponent of keeping the diocese and its churches in TEC.

An article in the Sept. 25, 2003, Episcopal News Service Archive, for example, quoted the bishop as saying, "We have not voted in any way to sever our relationship with The Episcopal Church, USA. Nor, I hope, will we ever do so."

Moving on down the road

Assisting handicapped sibling parishioners Norman and Carol Turner was, by all accounts, a main outreach program of Holy Trinity during much of the 1990s and for several years thereafter. The Turners lived in Wildwood, and various members of the congregation were involved in cleaning their home, maintaining their yard and bringing them to Fruitland Park , about nine miles away, for services. Largely in response to the latter task, the church decided in 1997 to buy a van.

Vestry minutes indicate that some of the money for the purchase came from a benefit and some (in 1998) from Bob Freeman's work at a Disney concession for 10% of its profits. In addition, said John Buzzell, "A few of our people went down to the (Orlando) Magic games and sold hot dogs."

The minutes show that the van, a 12-passenger Chevrolet model, was acquired in 1999 for $10,500.

Holy Trinity owned this vehicle for just three years before selling it to Jas Tyler, John's twin brother, for $5,000. At that time, according to Donna Bott, the church acquired a similar but better equipped unit through a grant from the United Thank Offering (UTO) that was written and submitted by the ECW.

(According to John Tyler, once Jas acquired the original van, he used it to transport children for the Kids' Depot, a day care center he operated in Wildwood.)

Buzzell said that he was unwilling to drive a 12-passenger van but regularly accompanied John Tyler on trips to the Turner residence. "John would drive the van and I would go along with him and operate the lift," Buzzell pointed out.

That second van, named Barnabus, remained in Holy Trinity's ownership until shortly after Hurricane Katrina hit the Gulf Coast in 2005. At that time, the vestry decided to donate the vehicle to the Diocese of Mississippi. Barnabus was loaded with emergency supplies, and Brad Ingalls drove it to Mississippi with several other parishioners also making the trip.

Blessing Barnabus
Left to right: Norman Turner, Chuck Buohl, The Rev. Paul Heckters, Dorothy Heckters, Lillian Hammond, Mother Meg Ingalls, Peggy Hoe, and Lorraine Ullery.

In explaining the contribution, Donna Bott said, "The (UTO) grant was written on the premise that more and more people would be utilizing the van. It was used for transportation from time to time to go to a diocesan convention but not really what it should have been, and the insurance was killing us. We responded out of need – for them and for us!"

Both Bott and Buzzell noted that the Diocese of Mississippi was very appreciative of the gift. As far as they know, the van is still in use there.

The Turners now live in Ocala, and Parker and Charlotte Bauer periodically drive them to church by private car.

Bott remarked that the Turners are also why Holy Trinity acquired wheelchairs which continue to be of benefit to others as well.

To the millennium . . . and beyond

Following an absence of several years, beginning immediately after Meg Ingalls' appointment as rector, a long-time fixture at Holy Trinity was resurrected for a period.

"We did not have anyone running an ECW (Episcopal Church Women) for some time and then Lucille Michaels came along," Ingalls explained. "She got busy and started working to revitalize the group. She did a great job. She got it up and running with a really good board that supported the activities. It really began to run very, very well . . . Then Jean Buatti was the real guiding force for some time. She served as ECW president." Eventually, however, the people who ran it began to run out of steam, although they still did projects and they still did the cookie sale at Christmas, the annual yard sale, and the chili sale for Super Bowl Sunday.

The group disbanded in the spring of 2007 and has not been re-established.

The last year of major youth attendance and involvement at Holy Trinity, accounts indicate, was 1998. "That was the big year," Ingalls remarked. "We had 13 seniors who graduated and they left fewer behind them. We still had a youth group but it was not as well formulated as the group that had preceded that 1998 group. By that time The Villages was really beginning to exert its demographics into Holy Trinity."

Within just a couple of years, the vestry considered hiring a youth minister but no action was taken; there were essentially no children in the church. This situation continues to the present.

In 2006, in an attempt to address this matter, the church offered a short-lived "contemporary service" at 9 a.m. on Sunday. Officiated by David Dawkins, a seminarian at Suwanee, Tenn., until he left to return to his studies, this service was reportedly designed for youth and young families. In some ways it was a variant of a mid-1990s service requested by kids. The earlier version, Ingalls recalled, was attended by 20-some students and was held in the parish hall with "their music", a screen, and individuals taking turns leading. At that time the adults wanted the kids back with them; the youth refused unless their music was blended in. Ingalls said the adults promised to do so, then complained. It didn't happen, and the kids were upset.

A shortage of funds was again an issue on various occasions during this period.

For example, the minutes for one year note, "Deficit for 1998 to be covered by CD" and, for another, "the vestry understands that we are in financial difficulty."

"We always had deficits until the last few years," said John Buzzell. "We were always broke."

There are several assessments as to why finances appear to have improved somewhat recently with different people citing increased membership, slightly higher pledging and better money management.

Sometime in the late 1990s, and possibly at the suggestion of Meg Ingalls, a library was started in the parish hall. The collection included both religious and other books. Anne Smith and Lillian Labud were in charge. According to one parishioner, Smith, a retired librarian, "went to great lengths to catalog the books," but the library was hardly used. It was eventually discontinued and the books, many of which were quite dated, were given away in 2008.

The year 2000 was a big one for Holy Trinity's involvement with Habitat for Humanity. Vestry minutes state that church members raised $3,900 for the organization, much of it apparently coming from Lenten mite boxes. Volunteers from Holy Trinity collaborated with those from St. James in Leesburg, St. Edward's in Mount Dora, St. George in The Villages and St. Mary's in Belleview to build a home. Bob Freeman donated plumbing for the house.

The church publication "Tidings" on two instances in the fall of 2000 referred to the parish hall as "Joseph Julian Hall" after Holy Trinity's first priest. Apparently someone, possibly Ingalls, gave the facility that label about that time but that name has never actually been used.

That year ECW donated lights for the parish hall. Brad Ingalls was recommended for postulancy and entered Virginia Seminary in 2001.

Sharon Redding returned as music director in 2001 and has continued to the present. Kippy Benedict and then Janet Foster were her immediate predecessors in this role.

In 2002 Don Hooten developed the first web page for the church. ECW paid for carpeting for the parish hall and the vestry room. New keyboards – one for the church, the other for the choir room – were provided in memory of Bettie Pettie, and "Lift Every Voice" hymnals were purchased.

Several construction projects occurred in 2003 with the replacement of the septic tank being the biggest and most expensive. John Buzzell took charge of this project. One Sunday at both services he explained the situation, pointing out that $8,000 would have to be generated since the church had no other funds to cover the cost. The amount was raised in just two weeks!

Shellie Leon also added gardens to the church entrance area that year.

ECW fund raisers at that time included, along with those recently mentioned, a trash and treasure sale (an Ingalls-era follow-up to the May Festival) and a Valentine dinner party. In addition, a full-length play, "Seven Nuns in Las Vegas" drew standing room-only crowds for its two performances.

The church bylaws were revised and adopted by the parish but, according to the vestry minutes, never approved by the bishop.

Holy Trinity helps another start-up

In 2002, if not earlier, several events began that in some cases were unrelated but eventually came together to result in Holy Trinity's helping found what is today the mission of Corpus Christi in Okahumpka.

Some people at Holy Trinity, including Ingalls, were expressing concerns about its "survivability." Their fears were due, in part, to the church's somewhat rural location, its proximity to two big parishes (St. James in Leesburg and St. George in The Villages), and to general changes in the area's population. Undoubtedly different ideas were proposed, some of which had to do with membership count and with ongoing financial issues. One notion that was mentioned, but never got traction, was for the parish to build a new church on vacant land behind the school.

At the diocesan convention in January 2002 those in attendance, including members from Holy Trinity, heard a report on the demographics of the diocese. This account said Lake County was the fastest-growing county in the diocese and the area south of Leesburg was one of the current hot spots. Demographers didn't know this but The Daily Sun, The Villages' newspaper, had reported locally that the population of The Villages was expected to exceed 100,000 people by 2014.

In a motel room at the convention, local delegates began to discuss the idea of a multi-site church arrangement. According to Ingalls, "We said we're going to have to start thinking out of the box if we're going to help Holy Trinity to survive. We were feeling different sorts of pressures. We thought 'What if we develop a multi-campus church, had all the central administrative offices in one spot, and then had several different churches that we could host out of the central church?'"

That March Ingalls and then-senior warden Donna Bott invited Bishop Howe to visit and explore this concept with regard to The Villages. Construction of the retirement community's second town square, Lake Sumter Landing, had just started. The bishop encouraged continued exploration.

Ingalls presented the concept to the vestry and then to the parish in a series of sermons. In July, discussion of the multi-site approach took place at several town meetings at Holy Trinity. These events were organized by Bott for the various geographical areas served by the church. According to a related document (that was eventually used in a presentation to the congregation in January 2003), "While we were open to exploring multi-site as one possible solution to population growth, it was clear that there was concern for Holy Trinity's viability as well, and that there was a need to address both issues. Questions raised: Do we have the resources to start a new church? How can we ensure our historic Fruitland Park church will not be relegated to museum-like status, used only on special occasions, once there is a large new Holy Trinity church in Sumter County? How can our small congregation, with relatively modest resources, stay equal partners with a large congregation and its significantly greater resources?"

A multi-site task force was appointed and began meeting in September 2002. Members of this group were Rod Jones, Donna Bott,

Aelish Quayl, Shellie Leon, Don Hooten and Susy Brown. According to the previously mentioned document, one of the group's working assumptions was that "since the need for a new Episcopal church in Sumter County is primarily driven by the projected 32,000 new homes in The Villages, the first choice location of the new church should be in The Villages' new Sumter County development."

The task force soon found that "Temporary space for conducting worship services in The Villages is contingent upon having purchased property from The Villages for constructing a new church . . . There is currently no property available for church construction in The Villages. We have been encouraged to contact them again this summer. We are also looking at the option of nesting with another congregation as a temporary place of worship."

The document, which was the final report of the task force, concludes, "We have time to continue examining the issues surrounding multi-site, including the preferred option of locating within the new Villages development. The targeted population for whom the church is needed is not here yet and will not be here in significant numbers for at least a year or more."

Holy Trinity's second Faith Alive weekend occurred shortly thereafter in 2003. (As reported earlier, the first such weekend had taken place in 1982.) This was perhaps the most significant event of that year, one that initially was unrelated to the multi-site discussion.

According to its website, Faith Alive features "stories of faith bring(ing) fresh focus to how one's vows of baptism provide a formula for living a life pleasing to God. No teaching, no preaching, no church politics; simply faith-building worship and the sharing of answered prayers and similar experiences of God's love."

Faith Alive's site lists its attributes:

"With an emphasis on spiritual renewal, introduces small-group ministry which can be continued after the weekend through small-group Bible studies and prayer & share groups;

"Is a catalyst to help launch new lay ministries in your parish;

"Is a great way to kick off a program of congregational development and revitalization."

Bott explained that the 2003 Faith Alive weekend came about following her assignment to evangelism and outreach after being elected to the vestry. She knew about this program and, with vestry approval, arranged for it to take place.

Ingalls said, "At the end of the weekend, I remember that we all gathered in the parish hall and out of that came a request that we do more groups like we had done that weekend. We had been in people's houses. We began to say that we will develop house churches which had been in my mind since the mid-90s. This was the opportunity to do that."

Three groups, all of which, Ingalls said, had differing approaches, sprang from this weekend. Two met in homes.

The first was Bott's POTS (Prayer on the Square, at Spanish Springs in The Villages), a version of which continues to this day. Ann's Angels, moderated by Ann Fisher, was the second. This group, which disbanded following Fisher's death, mostly comprised the Fruitland Park women, Ingalls noted. And finally, the priest said, "we had the people who were on the southern end of our congregation, down around the Plantation and that area. They called themselves the Southern Saints."

While the Faith Alive groups were beginning to blossom, nothing further happened with multi-site prospects within or near The Villages. Holy Trinity and the diocese lacked the monetary resources to make the purchase, especially since land in that area was being sold at a premium, and neither entity could provide the needed financial support if property was acquired. In addition, the site needed to be golf cart accessible, further complicating the situation.

Ingalls noted, "We started watching as the Southern Saints were really growing. They got to the point where they didn't really want to separate and become two house churches. They wanted to continue as a single house church. So it looked like they would be the best bet to become the first of hopefully more than one site away from the mother church (Holy Trinity).

"They started looking for a place to meet . . . Eleanor Howarth said, 'I think I may have found a place. She and I went to see it – a restaurant (connected with the Angelina Motel, south of Leesburg on US 27). We found out that one of the Southern Saints actually worked for the woman who owned the building which was just kind of one of those God things. The owner was willing to let us have it for $500 a month." (Of course that charge didn't include clean-up and refurbishing it into a worship space.) According to vestry minutes, the finding and preparation of the building and the congregation's moving in happened in 2004.

"We had money from the Frame estate that we had always used for outreach projects," Ingalls said. "We decided to use that money until the Southern Saints could raise enough money to take over paying their portion down there. So it wasn't going to come out of the general fund."

One of the other big concerns with this new arrangement was its governance. Ingalls explained how that began to be handled. "The year before we actually started to move into the (restaurant) space . . . we decided to rewrite the bylaws. So Rod Jones took on the responsibility to create a committee to do that. They came up with a very good set (which was never approved by the diocese) . . . We wanted as much parity as we could get but not so much that the baby would overwhelm the mother . . . So it seemed to be going OK but one of the problems that began to happen is that it became an 'us vs. them' kind of a situation."

All Saints Chapel

The Rev. Arthur Bradford Ingalls

Ingalls continued, "We started calling Holy Trinity 'Grace Chapel' so there would be a feeling of parity there. [She apparently promoted 'Grace Chapel' because that was the name of a small, part-time forerunner of Holy Trinity in the 1880s when Fruitland Park was called Gardenia.] Then we had All Saints Chapel (the name adopted by the Southern Saints) with both being parts of Holy Trinity, the church."

Ingalls husband, Brad, who had been ordained a priest by then, was assigned to serve the new facility.

It was All Saints that, by mutual agreement, would become a separate entity from Holy Trinity a few years later, move to Okahumpka and become Corpus Christi Episcopal Church.

A capital idea

Where a 120-year-old church building is concerned, repairs and upgrades are discussed frequently and are an ongoing issue. However, in 2005, conversations at Holy Trinity started to become more substantial and eventually resulted in a major capital operation that became known as the Heritage Campaign.

Following some initial talks and planning, a committee was formed in 2006 to lead the campaign. This group consisted of chairman Michael Rowell; John Buzzell, Russ Casson (soon to become co-chair), Buster Evertson, Jacquie Guernsey, Rod Jones (campaign coordinator), Sharon Redding and Meg Ingalls. The committee, eventually working in conjunction with a consultant from the New York-based Episcopal Church Foundation, decided that the campaign should concentrate on six major areas: the exterior of the church building and the parish house, the interior of the church building, the refinishing of the church building and the rectory floors, the renovation of several other areas of the rectory, the paving of the parking lot (which ultimately became the top priority), and the purchase of a new organ. The projected cost to do everything was $230,635.

In 2007, prior to the campaign actually getting underway, crossover singer Peter Donnelly performed a concert to raise funds. Then a kick-off dinner at Colony Cottage Recreation Center in The Villages took place in February 2008 and pledges were sought over a several-month period. Pledges could be paid outright or spread over three years but ultimately came in, according to vestry minutes, at $168,000, appreciably short of the goal. As it turned out, though, all six of the objectives were accomplished by Nov. 2, 2009, All Saints Day and the Sunday the organ was dedicated. This was a year ahead of schedule—and there was even some money left. Prompt payment of pledges and a lot of hands-on help by parishioners were key in making this feat possible. (For example, Jerry Wang and Emil Pignetti did just about all the work in the rectory.)

Parish hall interior

An extensive, eight-week renovation of the parish hall, where historical items would be displayed, was also completed during this period. Not really part of the campaign, this project was financed by individual donors. John Storey was the major restorer; he was assisted by many others. Shellie Leon, with considerable help as well, headed up the painting of the kitchen and the choir room. Church women served lunches while the work was underway.

After the campaign began, a proposal was made that congregants at All Saints be allowed to designate their pledges for the purchase of land for a permanent building for their church. This recommendation did not sit well with many people at Grace (as Ingalls and others then called Holy Trinity), and there were suggestions that allowing it could undermine the potential success of the operation. The vestry minutes for 2007 make comment about this matter, stating that when members were surveyed about the campaign, there were negative remarks about All Saints receiving funds, that Grace members were confused about All Saints, that there was never a plan nor a full explanation for that chapel, and that it would be better off as a mission. Although these assessments did not prevent the campaign from going forward, it was eventually determined that All Saints would become a separate entity by Dec. 31, 2007.

Delegates from the new chapel met with the bishop's assistant, Canon Ernie Bennett, to discuss becoming a mission of the diocese. As that congregation was facing a steep increase in its rent at the restaurant, from $500 to $2,500 per month, the old First Baptist Church of Okahumpka became available and, with a loan from the diocese, All Saints was able to purchase that building.

Ingalls recalled, "At the very end of 2007, one of the last services that we did was the commissioning service to send them out to do their work . . . We got them a new church register and everyone who was a member of Holy Trinity who was also now going to what would become Corpus Christi, I put them into their new book and removed them as members from Holy Trinity so that they could start out with their new book at their new place."

Corpus Christi Episcopal Church

The Rev. Deacon Karen House

Corpus Christi, the name of the congregation's choosing, was officially recognized as a mission at the diocesan convention in January 2008 with the Rev. Donald Gross named as priest-in-charge and Jacquie Guernsey as deacon. Gross was a retired priest affiliated with Holy Trinity and a teacher/chaplain at the school, and Guernsey, as previously noted, was also from Holy Trinity. In addition, Karen House was assigned as deacon at the new church after her ordination. The Rev. Amanda Wilson is now the vicar. Corpus Christi is presently growing and thriving.

And meanwhile . . .

As would be expected, while the Faith Alive groups were getting up and running, the whole multi-site scenario was playing out and the Heritage Campaign was underway, other things were taking place as well.

The possibility of building a new church on unused land surfaced again in 2004, according to the vestry minutes, and again this idea went nowhere.

That year was referred to in the minutes as "the year of the hurricanes;" the roofs of both the church and the parish house were replaced.

Ingalls' daughter, Sarah Ingalls Sutton, was nominated for the discernment process for the priesthood.

Member name tags were introduced in 2005, and a member hot line was established to allow for more electronic communication and less reliance on "Tidings" and bulletins for such things as pastoral needs, church events and updates.

A golf ministry, initially called the Holy Tees and now the Holy Hackers, was "the hit of the season," according to vestry minutes. There was a $2 per person fee at each outing that was given to Episcopal Relief and Development. This activity, currently headed by Pat McLaughlin, is going strong as of this writing and has had as many as 36 participants in the high season. According to one of its regulars, Donna Bott, "It's a great mixer for new and old members as well as early and late service folks." The fees now go to the school for its golf program. Janet Dearcopp headed up the school program, assisted by some of the Tee/Hacker golfers. Bott added, "Every May those kids now play with the Hackers. It's really a big deal for all of us."

On Dec.13, 2006, Holy Trinity commemorated the 120th anniversary of its founding with a special homecoming service and celebration. Ingalls used an 1894 chanted Evening Prayer (Evensong) and a dinner followed with the church packed.

A very destructive tornado hit the area on Groundhog Day in 2007. A number of members were affected, and four families were assisted financially. The disaster took the life of teenager Brittany May; she is buried in the churchyard.

In the aftermath of the tornado, Holy Trinity received $43,794 from the diocese and Episcopal Relief Development. A decision was made to spend this money on a Habitat for Humanity home. Habitat selected a Paisley family as the recipient for this house. Annette Freeman agreed to head up the Holy Trinity involvement. Many members worked on this project every Saturday through completion.

The most recent beach retreat weekend was held at Daytona Beach in 2007 with vestry member Donna Kelly in charge. This activity had occurred fairly regularly, always at Daytona, going back to the 1990s. From all indications, the events prior to 2007 were not real retreats but primarily social functions. John Tyler, who attended several, said they drew about 20-30 people. One thing he remembered: "On Sunday we would have service right on the beach. What was really neat was there would be people walking by on the beach and sometimes some of them would come by and join us."

(Tyler said that one year, when he couldn't attend, Meg Ingalls requested that he officiate at church while she and others were at the retreat. This led to his being asked on subsequent occasions, including several times for Janet Galbreath at Wednesday night Evening Prayer. "We didn't have a sermon on Wednesdays," Tyler said. "Wally Krzywicki would come in and play his little guitar, and we would sing songs." He also recalled one particular Wednesday when, like Ernie Davis at various mid-week services years earlier, "I arrived and there was nobody there. I did the whole thing anyway.")

Participation in the beach weekends was beginning to dwindle by the time Kelly went on the vestry. In 2007 she decided to organize a real retreat on contemplative prayer. Perhaps 30 or 35 people attended and the event met with a good reception. But the following year there seemed to be no real interest in any sort of retreat.

Brad Ingalls had left All Saints before it moved to Okahumpka to accept a call to Churchville, Md. His wife was granted a sabbatical at Holy Trinity for two months in early 2008. During this time, on January 29, she resigned after 15 years to become rector at the Church of the Transfiguration in Silver Spring, Md., where she is to this day. Her last service in Fruitland Park was on Sunday, March 2, 2008. The Rev. E. Michael Rowell was engaged as the interim beginning March 4.

Rowell, a native of Oklawaha and graduate of Florida State and the School of Theology at the University of the South, had previously been the rector in Albany, Ga., and Aiken, S.C. He lived in Naples before restoring his childhood home and moving back to this area in the mid-2000s.

The Rev. E. Michael Rowell

Much – but not all – of what happened during the remainder of 2008 at Holy Trinity involved deferred maintenance and custodial projects, effectively extensions of Heritage Campaign work. An unattributed quote in the vestry minutes sums up these efforts: "We will no longer tolerate dirt and grime, second-hand anything, or quick fixes. God deserves the very best as do all who enter through our doors, members and guests alike."

Interior of church

The vestry hired a cleaning service and, as noted in the minutes, a "massive" clean up/clean out took place. A new air conditioner was acquired for the sanctuary. The church was professionally painted with the door covered in "grenadine red." The kitchen and the choir room were redecorated. Recycling was initiated. An upgrade of the church interior was done in October.

Exterior of church

In happenings not involving maintenance, Rowell initiated the first Sunday forum in March and he and his wife, Amy, hosted the vestry and church newcomers at their home. The vestry hosted a dinner for school graduates, revised the cemetery rules and regulations and sold unused handbells to a parish in New Jersey with the proceeds going to the Heritage Campaign.

The church enlisted Lay Eucharistic Visitors (LEVs) for pastoral care and to work with the interim priest in taking the sacrament to the sick or homebound. The Rev. Sally Dover later became the pastoral care coordinator and was put in charge of making the assignments for the LEVs as well as arranging for other pastoral needs.

In a matter of significant consequence, following a real period of discernment involving a financial analysis and a well-attended town meeting, the vestry made a decision to call a part-time priest for Holy Trinity.

As 2009 began, the search committee for a new priest had been established. This group consisted of chairwoman Jeanette Schotta, Sheri Banks, Beverly Pignetti, Harold Topping, Julie Sligh, Rod Jones and Hugh Hughston. The committee developed a new parish survey/parish profile as a major step in the calling of Ingalls' successor. Over 100 people attended the annual meeting, and $126,000 was pledged, an increase of $33,000 over the previous year.

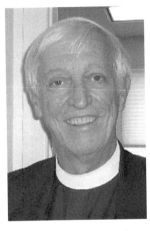

The Rev. Lawrence R. Recla

Renovation of the rectory was completed in 2009, and the new organ, paid for from Heritage Campaign funds, was dedicated on All Saints Day.

The Rev. Lawrence R. Recla, a retired ELCA (Evangelical Lutheran Churches of America) pastor, was selected as an interim beginning April 1. (The Episcopal Church is in communion with the ECLA.) Recla's term ended September 29.

Several other activities got underway at various times in the interval following Meg Ingalls' departure. They included the Sunday morning food bank contributions for the Leesburg Salvation Army and the Terry Colla-initiated prayer shawl ministry. Both are ongoing to this day. In addition, Annette Freeman started a stamp-trimming project for Habitat for Humanity that continues on a periodic basis.

Bott also gave presentations about the early history on several occasions to church and community audiences.

It was during this time that Holy Trinity adopted the theme "We are God's servants working together."

This "togetherness" carried over into social events. With Rob Michaels as chairperson, a committee put on such activities as a spring fling dance (with a DJ) in the courtyard, Mardi Gras and Oktoberfest celebrations and a retirement party for Michael Rowell. The group also started a December Dickens Dinner tradition.

Assessing these two years overall, one member pointed out, "This was a period of high energy."

Dancing in the courtyard replaces teas at the Bosanquets

Sometime after 8 p.m. on Monday, July 27, Holy Trinity sustained its first-ever act of substantial vandalism. Windows, glass doors, light fixtures, mirrors and assorted electronic items in the sanctuary, parish hall and the church and school offices were damaged. Ruth Mower, parish administrator, discovered and immediately reported the matter when she arrived for work just before 8 a.m. on Tuesday. The perpetrator did most of the nearly $7,000 in damage with a hammer. Fortunately, the only religious articles affected were the sanctuary lamp, which was shattered, and the baptismal font, which was pushed over.

Minus a $500 deductible, the church's insurance covered most of the cost for repair or replacement. Several parishioners also made financial contributions, and a number of others helped with clean-up and in other ways, This work was completed in reasonably short order with little effect on church activity.

According to Bott, who was the senior warden at the time, Holy Trinity had already contracted for a security system when the event occurred but the system had not yet been installed. She said that it is now in place and operative in all buildings.

Shortly after this incident, on August 12, a sterling chalice, paten and lavabo bowl were blessed in honor of Michael Rowell.

Dr. Hugh and Ruth Hughston donated a new identification sign for the church that is in place in Paddock Point near Spring Lake Road and the parking lot.

A sound system was acquired for the parish hall and, following the vandalism, the one in the church was upgraded.

The school was selected as the primary focus of Holy Trinity's parish outreach.

The Rev. Theodore Frank Koelln

In the fall of 2009, the vestry called the Rev. Theodore (Ted) F. Koelln to be the new priest-in-charge. He conducted his first service Nov. 29, 2009, the first Sunday in Advent. The celebration of a new ministry was held a few weeks later on Dec. 27.

Born in Boston, the new priest earned a bachelor's degree from South Dakota State University. He worked as a Zoning Enforcement Officer in Sioux Falls, S.D., before entering seminary in Suwanee, Tenn. After seminary Koelln served parishes in the Diocese of South Dakota and held two positions in the Diocese of Central Florida—as vicar at St. Luke the Evangelist Mission in Mulberry and as chaplain at All Saints Academy in Winter Haven. Then he became rector at Good Shepherd Episcopal Church in Decatur, Ala., where he served for five years prior to he and wife Pat coming to Holy Trinity.

Koelln sent the senior warden an e-mail response on the night he received his call to Fruitland Park. Part of this message reads as follows: "It is my earnest desire to come there and share with you all the love that God has called us to share. For me, that is what being a Christian family is all about – knowing that God loves us beyond our wildest imagination and then doing our very best to share that love with one another and with all we meet."

Holy Trinity has now been sharing that love for more than 120 years. God willing, it will be doing so for many more years to come.

Epilogue

NUMEROUS BUILDING and grounds projects, most having no connection with the Heritage Campaign, began after Fr. Ted Koelln was called.

The exception involved the courtyard; some renovations there, primarily landscaping and brick paver installation, commenced in September 2009 with funds left from the campaign. To "anchor" the courtyard, Hugh and Ruth Hughston donated a cross in 2010. Ellen Bosanquet lilies are planted around it. Dedication of the cross occurred on Trinity Sunday, June 19, 2011, as part of an observation of the 125th anniversary of Holy Trinity. A Victorian tea was also held in the parish hall to celebrate this event.

The indoor work occurred in the parish house. The first project, an upgrading of the sound and video systems, took place in late 2009. At that time the church purchased a 10-channel power mixer with 16" speakers, a cordless microphone and a lapel mike.

Then the restrooms were relocated in March 2010, a move that was necessitated by serious plumbing issues. That August the vestry determined that the old bathrooms would be converted to office space. This decision allowed the former rector's office to become a multi-function room/chapel, with the chapel aspect being for a Wednesday healing service that was initiated in 2008. A group of parishioners, led by junior warden Shellie Leon, did most of the work to create the new facility and to prepare the priest's new workplace. Both projects are now complete. The multi-function room features stained glass windows designed and made by participants in a stained glass class initiated by Koelln in July 2011 and taught by him. (One of the windows has an orange hidden in it!)

In June of 2010, the kitchen was completely remodeled and new air conditioning was installed.

The large classroom was partitioned in November 2010 with one section left as a smaller schoolroom and the other becoming a stained glass studio.

The vestry purchased a new white funeral pall in May 2009 and the following May replaced the air conditioner in the parish hall.

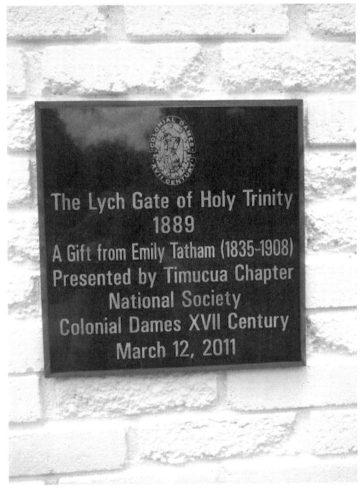

lych gate plaque

Ivan Ford and Donna Bott collaborated with Emil Pignetti and Rod and Kathy Jones on an eight-panel illustrated brochure that was completed in April 2010 as a precursor to this book. Entitled "A Brief History of Holy Trinity Episcopal Church: A story of sturdy faith, stable tradition and spirited optimism," the publication focuses on the years before 1900, the building itself, the church's furnishings and the cemetery. Copies were distributed to parishioners, to the Leesburg Heritage Society and to the Lake County Historical Society and are currently available in a display rack near the church entry door.

On March 12, 2011, the Timucua Chapter of the Colonial Dames Seventeenth Century conducted an historic marking ceremony of the lych gate at Holy Trinity. The event was held outdoors and was well attended. Afterward everyone went into the church for a short historical presentation by Donna Bott, one of several she gave during a two-year period to various audiences. The Timucua Chapter furnished a plaque which has since been installed by the gate.

A number of choir members of Holy Trinity volunteered to join with peers from St. George in The Villages to sing a Christmas cantata, "Night of the Father's Love," that December. There was a standing room-only audience for this event which was held at St. George.

In January 2011 Bishop Howe notified the diocese of his intent to retire in April 2012. He made his final official visit to Holy Trinity as bishop on March 4, 2012, baptizing one, confirming four and receiving six.

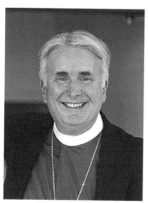

The Rt. Rev.
Gregory Oren Brewer

The Rev. Gregory Oren Brewer was consecrated as Howe's successor and the fourth bishop of the Diocese of Central Florida on March 24, 2012. He was the rector of Calvary-St. George's Church in New York City at the time of his election. Brewer, who earlier served in Central Florida for 16 years, was chosen on the fourth ballot from a field of seven.

The installation ceremony for the new bishop was held at the First Baptist Church in Orlando to accommodate the estimated 3,500 attendees. Representing

Holy Trinity were Koelln, Parker Bauer as an elected trustee of the University of the South, and Graham Sligh as the church's banner carrier.

Sligh is now a freshman at the University of Virginia. For the last several years, he was one of a very few young people regularly attending Holy Trinity. Active in church ministry throughout this period, he began as an acolyte and crucifer and then progressed to lector and Lay Eucharistic Minister.

The golf instruction program at Holy Trinity Episcopal School was discontinued during the 2011-12 school year. There are no plans for it to be resumed.

In mid-2011, Rob Michaels, who had been the driving force behind fellowship activities, resigned his involvement with Pat Koelln succeeding him. Michaels has since put his energies into encouraging participation by interested Holy Trinity members in the Tri-County (Lake, Marion and Sumter) Interfaith Alliance which, according to its coordinator, "has been meeting monthly to educate the public on the many religions in this country. The goal is to understand and accept that there are many faiths in this country and to respect others' faiths so that we can reduce prejudice, fear and ignorance, thereby learning to live together in harmony."

Lost but Found

THIS SECTION contains items that were discovered (in some cases uncovered) after the text was finalized for publication. For the most part they are placed here in the order of their occurrence.

More on the shadowboxes:

During Fred Paddock's tenure, as reported earlier, the original altar hangings, clerical stoles, and offering bags were sealed in shadowboxes that are now attached to the walls of the sanctuary. A clipping from the Oct. 11, 1972, Orlando Sentinel, provided by Dottie Paddock, gives a little more information about this matter. Written by Gail Bell and entitled "Embroidery Work of 1886 'Home' Again in a Church," the article says, "The monograms and symbols of Christianity were used to soften the rough interior of the Vickers-Smith barn of Zephyr Lake [actually Lake Geneva] which was being used as a temporary church." Up to this time the bags, et al, were stored in a cedar chest and brought out only for special occasions. (The) Paddocks arranged for preservation in the shadowboxes with the Minerva Art Gallery in Mount Dora who repaired some of the pieces. "The old and new blend here in a peaceful setting of trees and birds. The sisters . . . would be pleased to know their work of art is in its rightful place again, in the house of God for all to see."

Back to his roots:

As was explained previously, Fred Paddock came to Fruitland Park from the West Palm Beach area. He returned there to preach at the 20th anniversary of Holy Redeemer Church in nearby Lake Worth. As outlined in an unidentified newspaper clipping probably from 1980, "In his last year at seminary, when he was affiliated with Holy Trinity in West Palm Beach, he gathered together the first members of what was to become the Church of the Holy Redeemer and conducted its first services in a store on Lake Worth Road on July 10, 1960."

Regarding Paddock Point:

In the part about Fred Paddock, there is mention of the establishment of a park named for him. Max R. Hoffman, a member of Holy Trinity, donated the land, while William M. Thomson, Eleanor Thomson Thomas and Nancy Thomson Kranz, family and friends, were also responsible for the creation of the park.

Hoffman died before the facility was dedicated on Palm Sunday, April 12, 1981, and it was dedicated to his memory. He is buried in the churchyard.

His signature dismissal:

Dottie Paddock pointed out that at the conclusion of each Sunday service her husband always dismissed people with the Serenity Prayer.

Something to crow about:

Over the years Holy Trinity has had several cats who have already been mentioned in the coverage of the Ernie Davis years. And since the 1980s Susy Brown has fed and cared for them. However, during the time Meg Ingalls was here there was also a dog and even a rooster. The rooster's name was Roger. Like the cats, he just appeared in the churchyard one day and decided to stay. He was known for crowing right at 8 a.m. sharp to signal the beginning of the early service. Reportedly the schoolchildren loved him, and he was right in the middle of everything. One day he was hit by a car on Spring Lake Road. Ingalls dressed in vestments and held a funeral for Roger for the kids.

The dog was Molly; she belonged to Ingalls who often brought her to work.

Molly, and Jordan the cat (who was mentioned earlier), are now buried in the Rector's Garden on the north side of the parish office building. Roger rests under his roost, the tree outside the office.

At the time of this writing, the church was home to three cats – Samuel, Miss Kitty and Chester.

A special Holy Week contribution:

In the mid-2000's, Lenore Kramer contributed the Stations of the Cross that are now on the walls of the sanctuary at Holy Trinity.

Kramer, since deceased, was an active and faithful church member who at one time served on the vestry and on occasion led small group Bible studies.

An Ingalls tradition:

The following prayer was said at nearly every service during Meg Ingalls' tenure: "We rejoice to welcome those who have been brought here by the Holy Spirit. We give thanks for all the many blessings in our lives, especially those named by our congregation this day. [This was said in conjunction with the little white church offering (the Thank You, Lord offering) which was mentioned earlier in the text.] We give thanks that out of many, we are one holy people – preaching, teaching, reaching others in the name of our Lord. We vow to uphold this church with our prayers, our presence, our gifts and our service. We vow to be proponents of reconciliation, peacemakers in the midst of crisis, healers in the midst of pain, and bearers of Christ to all the world. Amen.

Appendix

Verified Founders of Holy Trinity Episcopal Mission

George R. Back
Augustus P. Bosanquet
Eugene P. Bosanquet
Louis P. Bosanquet
Hugh S. Budd
Alexander P. Cazalet
Robert F. E. Cooke
Francis R. L. Cosens
W. C. Earle Geary
Charles and Amanda Gomperts
Charles Gomperts Jr.
Clarence Gomperts
Gertrude Gomperts
Laura Gomperts
Jonathan and Maria Josephine Luther
James and Rose Jane Routledge
Elizabeth Smith
James Vickers and Mary Smith
John Vickers Smith
Margaret Smith
Sarah Smith
Villiers Chernocke Smith
Granville and Elizabeth Stapylton
Kenneth R. S. Streatfield
Ernest B. Thomson
Thomas A. Vincent
Wilfred P. P. Western

Priests and Senior Wardens

Priests

1886-1887 John Campbell Wheatley Tasker
1888-1892 Joseph Ernest Julian
1893-1894 James Taylor Chambers
1895-1896 A. Kinney Hall
1897-1898 Joseph M. McGrath
1898-1899 James Neville Thompson
1900-1901 William Johnson
1902-1905 Clarence M. Frankel
1905-1906 S. W. Moran
1907 A. Rickers
1908-1911 Aykroyd Stoney
1912-1921 George Henry Ward
1922-1927 Francis J. Wilson
1928-1939 Randolph Fairfax Blackford
1939-1942 Frank E. Pulley
1942-1945 James H. MacConnell
1945-1950 William Martin Hargis
1950-1955 Lloyd Ashley Cox
1952-1960 Herbert Edson Covell
1961-1981 Frederick Norris Paddock
1982-1985 William H. Walters
1985-1991 Ernest Percival Davis
1993-2007 Margaret Eileen Fowler Ingalls
2009- Theodore Frank Koelln

Senior Wardens

1887 Granville Chetwynd Stapylton
1892 John Vickers Smith
1892 Villiers Chernocke Smith
1924 Louis Percival Bosanquet
1930 Alfred Percival Bosanquet
1949 Edwin Ruser
1950 William Rumley
1953 Nathan Wall
1954 Ernest R. Hastings
1955 Ormond Vickers-Smith
1958 Dr. Bradford Spencer
Wesley C. Doyle, Sr.
1961 Fred C. W. Kramer, III
1963 Robert M. Braun
1965 Lawrence K. Casson
1966 Robert Fallin
1967 Gershon Percival Bosanquet
1968 Theodore White, Jr.
1969 William Fowler
1970 Dr. M. M. Tutton
1971 Richard Sutherland
1972 Morris Bays
1973 Ted Reames
William Fowler
1974 Ron Cartledge
1975 Bill W. Martin
1976 William B. Morrow
1977 Paul Duszik
1978 James Rabon
1979 Perry Nichols
1980 Helen Peterman
1981 Chuck Herkal
1982 C. O. Raban
1983 Larry Sekker

1984 Barbara Faunt
1986 Jack Killmeyer
1987 Alex Peterman
1988 Nancy Faine
1989 Gershon Percival Bosanquet
1990 Janet Galbreath
1991 Susy Brown
1992 Gershon Percival Bosanquet
Janet Galbreath
1993 Janet Galbreath
1994 Greg Beleveau
1995 Annette Freeman
1996 John Tyler
1997 Jean Buatti
1998 Robert Updike
1999 Robert Freeman
2001 Susy Brown
2002 Donna Bott
2004 Barbara Pruitt
2006 Rick Unger
2007 Lawrence K. Casson II
2008 Donna Bott
2010 Harold Topping
2011 Sheri Banks
2012 Neil Groty

Holy Trinity Episcopal Church Cemetery

Fruitland Park, Florida
December 31, 2009

LAST NAME	FIRST NAME	MIDDLE NAME/S	BIRTH	DEATH
Abbott	Robert	Bernard Jr.	02/08/54	11/11/1973
Abbott	Dorothy	Ramistella	2/21/1933	4/7/1974
Abbott	Robert	Bernard Sr.	2/2/1929	9/2/1996
Abbott	Clifton	Robert	1904	1976
Adams	Bradford	G.M.	4/3/1901	10/22/1980
Adams	Henrietta	F.	10/13/1894	5/6/1973
Alexander	Willis	Elmer	3/4/1897	5/22/1979
Atkinson	Philip	D.	1929	1992
Atkinson	Juanita		1926	1991
Avery	Alice	Rice Davenport	11/26/1916	4/11/1988
Ayres	James	Walter	1922	5/7/1997
Bailey	Gordon	Wonnacott	1902	1991
Bailey	Thelma	Lee	1916	1993
Barber	Kenneth	Leon	6/21/1925	1/16/1979
Barber	Joyce	L.	08/18/29	6/27/1998
Barnes	Samuel	Alexander	1896	1980
Barnes	Katharine	D.	1897	1998
Bays	Murial		1922	1998
Bays	William	LeRoy	1913	1993

LAST NAME	FIRST NAME	MIDDLE NAME/S	BIRTH	DEATH
Bedsole	Katharine	Wolf	1948	1991
Benner	Frances	A.	1932	2000
Benner	Scott	W.	1960	1986
Benoit	Charles	Henry	1902	1985
Berry	Lucy	Hood	1876	1970
Berry	Frederick		1866	1934
Bishop	Richard	A	04/20/37	2/12/1983
Blackford	Rev. Randolf	F.	7/25/1890	7/19/1975
Blackford	Ellen	S. (Ford)	3/14/1882	9/4/1962
Blair	Gladys	Margaret	4/9/1906	2/27/1996
Blair	Howard	C.	5/13/1907	4/17/1997
Bond	Joseph	A.	1909	1982
Borst	Marylou		06/16/30	5/1/2004
Bosanquet	Louise		4/28/1895	1/21/1933
Bosanquet	Ellen	Lewis	1860	01/22/31
Bosanquet	Louis	Percival	1865	04/19/30
Bosanquet	Alfred	Percival	3/20/1897	5/3/1982
Bosanquet	Ruth	Ward	1902	1977
Bosanquet	Gershon	Percival	1934	1992
Bosanquet	Janis	King	1934	1991
Bova	Alma	Carol	1926	2003
Braden	Walter	Eugene Sr.	10/16/34	8/12/2001
Brown	James	Henry David	03/17/08	8/3/1993
Brunjes	Blanche	Goodridge	11/6/1875	06/11/77
Burd	Howard	Carl	NIL	1994
Burkhardt	Walter	Eugene	1905	1971
Burkhardt	Mary	Ruth (Britt)	1909	1974
Carey	Frances	J. (Jane)	1862	1960
Carr	Anna	K	1912	1995
Carroll	Wilson	Harold	4/5/1913	9/16/1999
Carroll	Leah	Maxine	11/14/1914	9/22/2004
Casson	Lawrence	Kenneth II	9/13/1951	9/7/2009
Casson	Lawrence	Kenneth Sr.	02/28/16	8/20/2002

LAST NAME	FIRST NAME	MIDDLE NAME/S	BIRTH	DEATH
Casson	Mary	Elizabeth	04/29/13	09/22/04
Catrambone	James	D.	1911	1977
Clark	Walter	Edward	1887	1943
Clark	Mildred	Kendrick	1891	1964
Congdon	Benjamin	Osgood	1883	1971
Congdon	Esther	Parker	1906	1975
Cook	Jeanne	Wolford	6/13/1911	02/02/95
Cook	Sam	Salisbury	3/12/1912	12/25/1990
Coombs	Richard	Carne	1894	12/01/58
Coombs	Edgar	Thomas	1890	11/06/71
Courington	Virginia	Worrall	01/03/09	12/4/2005
Courington	Wilton	Robert	1906	1972
Covell	Rev. Herbert	Edson	1/23/1880	1/23/1964
Cox	Juanita	Ivy	08/10/13	4/18/1998
Cox	Rev. Lloyd	Ashley	05/27/10	7/20/1982
Crossley	Marie	Eleanor	09/14/13	10/23/2001
Crossley	Robert	Henry	1919	5/27/1987
Curnow	Frances	Marion Olson	1908	8/10/2000
Davenport	Harry	N.	1876	1925
Davenport	Julia	Andrae	1876	1937
Davies	Edward		1898	1967
Davis	Ivy		1917	1985
Davis	Christian	D.	1907	1979
Davis	Lester	A., Sr.	1928	1994
Davis	Charles	Jefferson	8/13/1890	3/23/1987
Davis	Gail	Abbott	1934	1992
Dempsey	John	G.	1923	1967
Dempsey	Marian	MacPhee	1923	1967
Doyle	Wesley	Charles Jr.	09/27/16	9/16/2002
Doyle	Wilda	Grace	06/08/16	5/13/2002
Dubeck	Platon		1913	5/18/1976
Dubeck	John	Ludlow	02/16/43	3/20/1974
Dubeck	Frances	Seabright	1947	1974

LAST NAME	FIRST NAME	MIDDLE NAME/S	BIRTH	DEATH
Dunham	Helen	Asenath	1904	1993
Dunham	Mary	Capron	1882	1974
Duszik	Eugene	F.	1912	1985
Duszik	Frances	H.	1912	1992
Duvarney	Albert		05/27/20	2/28/1987
Dwyer	Frances	L.	11/17/09	11/12/1997
Ellsworth	Mary	Emma	11/29/1861	3/10/1936
Elsheimer	Clarence	William	1890	1976
Elsheimer	Sara	Jeanette Coulter	1895	1978
Emlich	Justin	N.	06/28/11	11/3/2000
Emlich	Lillian	H.	04/08/16	7/3/2006
Esch	Earl	Herbert	05/20/11	10/27/1984
Esch	Nelle	Elizabeth	11/12/11	3/20/1997
Fansler	Woodrow		1917	1991
Faunt	Claude	Richard	1918	1975
Faunt	Barbara	Christine	1934	7/19/1989
Finney	Doyle	Brooks	1938	1978
Fisher	Ann	Gridley	1931	06/09/08
Fisher	Joe	Allen	08/30/31	1/12/2000
Fiske	Lillian	M.	04/06/75	9/14/1966
Flowers	Melanie	Wheelock	06/26/60	8/5/2007
Foley	Lawrence	E.	1922	1971
Fowler	William	George	1923	4/26/1981
Frame	Eleanor	Eaton	1884	1965
Frame	William	Alexander	1880	1948
Fuller	Helen	L.	1912	1978
Fuller	Howard	James	1901	1985
Fullerton	Frances	German Amend	1910	1982
Gilchrist	Stuart			2007
Gilchrist	Louise	Bailey	1897	1966
Gerard	Diane		1925	1994
Gerard	William		1913	1997
Glasscock	Buford	LaRue	11/07/32	5/12/1995

LAST NAME	FIRST NAME	MIDDLE NAME/S	BIRTH	DEATH
Gomperts	Laura	Estelle	1870	1953
Gomperts	Amanda	Raymond	3/21/1847	5/24/1910
Gomperts	Charles		3/5/1840	2/13/1914
Goodridge	Harriet	Porter	1852	1939
Goodridge	Henry	W.	8/1/1844	1936
Goodridge	Marjorie	Hope	05/15/16	4/5/1992
Goodridge	George	Thomas Sr.	01/31/09	7/16/1995
Gorroll	Helen	Giannotti	1917	11/23/2006
Gorroll	Joseph	Michael	1906	1999
Graves	Hartley	Andrew Jr.	08/20/21	6/3/2004
Graves	Ione	Holloway	10/02/23	9/14/1997
Gridley	Adrian	Tipple Jr.	12/12/30	11/8/1982
Guernsey	Floyd	J.	08/29/29	11/25/2004
Hall	Liston	Fleming	1901	1982
Hall	Elizabeth	North	1908	1996
Hamilton	Florence		1912	1987
Hamm	C.	A.	10/6/1872	1/28/1935
Hamm	Ernestine	Johnson	1876	8/30/1876
Hammond	Phillip	L.	11/08/22	6/16/1998
Hanford	George	Arthur	11/7/1881	1/26/1956
Hanford	Cornelia	May	11/07/26	10/28/1936
Hanford	Ethel	W.	10/14/1893	6/20/1967
Hanford	Irene	A.	04/15/28	5/20/2006
Hanford	Charles B.	Jim	1924	1990
Hanson	Kenneth	W.	07/16/12	4/21/1999
Hanson	Alma	Wall	06/19/13	12/27/1996
Hardesty	James	William	08/22/22	2/12/1991
Harrell	Glenda		1911	1996
Hartwell	Lenora	Wallace (Ury)	1859	1937
Hartwell	Julius	H.	1848	1932
Hastings	Ernest	R.	1900	1998
Hastings	Gertude	Dean	1916	1993
Heckters	Paul	A.	05/28/21	3/6/2005

LAST NAME	FIRST NAME	MIDDLE NAME/S	BIRTH	DEATH
Hines	Winifred		1/10/1898	11/6/1976
Hines	Roderick	Thomas	12/08/12	12/20/75
Hines	Edith	M.	10/09/14	5/14/2005
Hoffman	Max	R.	1896	1981
Horan	William	Lytton	11/05/25	9/26/2005
Humbert	Howard		?/?/1909	?/?/1993
Hunter	Dr. Melville	Gunby	1900	1979
Hunter	Grace	Richmond	1906	1945
Hux	E.	W. Huxie	1916	11/23/1985
Hyslop	Samuel		1903	1997
Hyslop	Lucille	Rowan	1934	1999
Hyslop	Marjorie	A.	1911	2003
Hyslop	Robert	A.	04/17/36	12/29/2004
Jackson	Charles	Lawrence		1952
Jeffcoat	Helene	M.	1926	4/4/1998
Jeffcoat	Samuel	Walter (Jeff)	1921	1991
Johnston	Celia		11/7/1888	11/15/1972
Johnston	Charles	L.	6/7/1871	1/14/1952
Jones	Elizabeth	M.	1908	1993
Jones	Lloyd	M.	1903	1977
Julian	Sara	Brewster	1843	1936
Julian	Rev. Joseph	Ernest	1840	9/7/1892
Kay	Mathilda		1884	1977
Kelly	James	Frederick	1905	1977
Kelly	Gertrude	Elfrieda Schimmy	1924	2000
Kendrick	Mary	Goodridge	1865	1947
Kendrick	William	J.	1861	11/10/1935
Kerr	William	Alexander	1876	1948
Kerr	Mary	Frame	1870	1942
Kramer	Charles		1950	1950
Kramer	Geneva	Lukens		9/11/1980
Kramer	Frederick	Charles William III		12/10/2009
Kramer	Winifred		2000	11/17/2000

LAST NAME	FIRST NAME	MIDDLE NAME/S	BIRTH	DEATH
Langbein	Frances	Belle Pehl	1906	1977
Leo	Dora	Freeman	1920	4/21/2000
Leo	John	Joseph	1917	1991
Leo	Naino		02/17/13	9/23/1973
Lowe	Jean	Windram	11/09/26	3/28/2007
Lowe	Charles (Buddy)	LeRoy	08/25/26	11/13/2008
Ludlow	Rev. Ogden	R.	1919	9/12/2001
Luther	Beverly	Hail	12/24/1863	03/19/82
Lyle	Clifton		1909	1989
Lyle	Thelma		1910	1979
Lytle	Ernest	James	1867	1955
Lytle	Caroline	Pasteur	1888	1975
Lytle	Daniel	Wayne	1944	1946
Lytle	Florence	George	1914	1980
Lytle	Ernest	James, Jr.	06/28/13	10/3/1988
Lytle	John	Carney	09/19/15	8/30/1997
Lytle	Marian	Hoolehan	12/14/15	3/29/2003
Marcotte	Evelyn	Dorothy	1904	1986
Marcotte	Leo	A.	?/?/1905	?/?/1966
Mason	Charles	LeRoy	04/14/13	6/5/1983
May	Brittany	Anne	11/08/89	2/2/2007
McClain	Bradford (Rusty)	Ralph	06/04/38	4/5/1970
McClain	James	Murdoch	12/31/49	2/29/1996
McKenzie	Eric	Dale	08/31/64	10/9/2009
McNair	James	Edward Parry	1895	1982
McNair	Mary	Eileen Carmony	1897	1974
McNair	Hugh	Noel	06/06/01	9/23/1987
McNair	Dorothy	Mildred Trelawney	4/9/1897	3/8/1992
Meahl	Elmer	Dale	1921	1986
Meanor	Sara	Jane Bond	1912	
Michel	Frederick	Emil	03/12/23	11/18/2007
Michel	Audrey	Routson	07/03/22	5/31/2004
Mogg	Herbert	Braddock	1925	1980

LAST NAME	FIRST NAME	MIDDLE NAME/S	BIRTH	DEATH
Mogg	Betty	P.	09/07/22	3/26/1996
Mogg	Herbert (Chip) .	W.	10/16/52	3/30/1994
Monroe	Paul	Clark	1901	10/11/1962
Monroe	William	F. Jr.	05/11/24	11/10/1990
Monroe	William	F. Sr.	1900	1987
Muldoon	William	James	3/8/1894	6/9/1967
Muldoon	B.	Ruth	08/12/02	3/14/1967
Munson	Ruth		07/20/14	2/16/1999
Munson	Joseph		08/11/15	9/12/1998
Murphy	Jewell		06/07/08	1/17/2006
Murphy	Nevaeh	Ann	2003	2003
Newell	William	Reed	5/22/1868	4/1/1956
Newell	Mellicent	Woodworth	8/8/1870	8/22/1935
Newell	Betty	Washington	02/11/23	7/9/1926
Newell	Frances	Bosanquet	12/16/1892	9/9/1969
Newell	David	McCheyne	03/23/98	9/26/1986
Newell	Nancy	Ayers	1924	2000
Nicodem	Virginia	Mae	11/05/03	3/19/2000
Nipper	Letha	M.	12/18/12	2/2/1983
Nipper	Calvin	A.	03/17/05	12/4/1958
O'Brien	Allan		?/?/1920	1920
O'Brien	Malcolm	B.	1889	1970
O'Brien	Marjorie		1895	1987
O'Kelley	Marion	Benson	1904	1969
O'Kelley	Barbara	Hoffman	1913	1985
Paddock	Mary	Norris	1892	1983
Paddock	Rev.Frederick	Norris	11/20/19	11/22/1986
Pape	Paul (Bud)	C.	05/31/53	2/3/1992
Pape	Leona	Lynn	6/30/1899	3/31/1985
Peacock	George		8/26/1886	5/16/1974
Peacock	Mary	May	3/17/1887	11/14/1976
Peacock	Harriet		1889	6/4/1968
Peacock	Kathryn		11/7/1878	11/19/1973

LAST NAME	FIRST NAME	MIDDLE NAME/S	BIRTH	DEATH
Pearson	Charles	M. H.	8/20/1898	11/3/1976
Pearson	Edith	Dudley	12/31/06	9/6/1979
Perkins	Arthur	W.	1874	3/20/1894
Perkins	Stanley		?/?/1870	4/17/1894
Perry	Ella	Grace	12/05/04	3/2/2005
Perry	Benjamin	F.	1925	1987
Pettie	Elizabeth	Billingsley	?/?/1921	3/22/2002
Phelps	Raymond	Alton	1921	?1981
Pierce	Robert	E.	11/9/1915	1990
Pierce	Virginia	Alison	9/17/1915	3/25/1984
Pierotti	Deborah	Susan	07/12/52	7/15/1983
Potter	Louis	G.	1892	1961
Potter	Mary	Ellen	1900	2/18/1987
Pratt	Nathaniel	Alpheus, Jr.	08/03/24	12/28/2001
Pybus	Edmund		1896	8/16/1896
Quackenbush	Edytha	M.	1908	1981
Quackenbush	John	P.	1908	1994
Ramistella	Henry	Ronald	1934	03/05/77
Redding	Irene	Ruby Binns	1906	1964
Redding	Emmett	Leroy	1900	1969
Redding	Jack	Eugene	1929	1972
Redding	Wilma	Hulse	1913	1966
Reynolds	Reginald	Stephen	1867	7/16/1926
Rice	John	Douglas	02/02/12	5/6/1948
Ridlon	Joseph	Millard	03/23/09	9/16/1969
Robbins	Floyd	P.	12/01/01	2/13/1981
Robbins	Magdalene	Newkirk	1904	3/19/1994
Roehl	Clifford	A.	1919	1/4/1987
Routson	Charles	Orval	5/12/1894	12/13/1970
Routson	Carrie	Bell	11/24/95	10/4/1985
Rowan	Lucille	Hyslop	09/06/34	7/28/1999
Rudd	Katherine		1898	1988
Rudd	William	Chapman, Sr.	1896	1964

LAST NAME	FIRST NAME	MIDDLE NAME/S	BIRTH	DEATH
Rumley	Mabel	S.	1888	1962
Rumley	William	J.	1891	1973
Ruser	Edwin	Arthur	1905	1972
Ruser	Isabel	Martin Stead	1907	1991
Russell	Lawrence	E. Sr.	02/19/19	9/26/2002
Russer	William	N.	1897	10/6/1970
Schemanske	Margaret	Lillian Roberts	11/02/19	6/5/2003
Schrock	Gene	Wendell	1928	1994
Schrock	Mary	Annette	?/?/1928	?/?/1987
Scott	Jane	Tyler	1929	1983
Scott	H.	Wayne	1927	1991
Seigler	Claude	Milo	1923	7/10/1986
Selfe	Lola	M.	1876	1948
Sendelbach	Valentine		1892	1970
Sendelbach	Dorothy	Kate Jones	1889	1972
Sharpe	Phyllis	E.	05/25/09	5/6/1981
Shriver	Georgette C.	C.	09/14/17	11/9/2003
Silke	Ruth	Trapini	03/31/08	9/9/2001
Simpson	Frances	Bosanquet	11/12/27	12/23/2002
Simpson	Roy	Edward Sr.	01/09/21	9/9/1997
Simpson	Roy	Edward Jr.	12/22/53	6/17/1984
Smith	James		1814	1887
Smith	Mary		1809	1890
Smith	Sarah	Jane	1842	1920
Smith	Margaret	Ann	1845	1927
Smith	Elizabeth	Mary	1850	1928
Smith	Eleanora	Thorburn	1869	1942
Smith	Ray	H.	03/06/23	12/14/1968
Smith	Geraldine	Robertson	06/03/15	07/07/94
Smith	John	Morris	12/28/09	11/30/1994
Smith	Lawrence	H.	1913	1976
Spencer	Bradford	J.	1890	1958
Spencer	Ada	Belle	1899	1972

LAST NAME	FIRST NAME	MIDDLE NAME/S	BIRTH	DEATH
St. John	Clarice		1867	1963
Staemler	Richard	Louis Sr.	1927	1986
Stead	Richard	John	1916	1994
Stead	Virginia		1921	1986
Teese	Robert	G.	07/11/05	12/23/79
Teese	Maude	Beard	05/05/07	11/22/1989
Tench	Samuel	Vandenburg	?/?/1905	?/?/1979
Thirsk	Olive	May	04/24/02	8/30/1986
Thirsk	Stanley	Potter	4/29/1896	9/8/1967
Thomson	Selina		1911	1998
Thomson	John		1904	1969
Tilbey	Peter	F.	1927	1999
Tilby	Dorothy	Ida	1894	1985
Trampish	Georgia		1913	2005
Trampish	Lawrence		1948	1992
Trampish	Norman		1913	1991
Turner	Carl		1900	1977
Turner	Doris	Willard	1903	1975
Tutton	Mather	Marvin	04/15/20	4/26/1982
Tutton	Penny	(Jean) Mogg	12/18/48	11/17/2008
Ury	Charles	E.	1/3/1889	1/20/1966
Ury	Walter	Wightman	10/22/27	1998
Ury	Edna		1/5/1892	11/3/1982
Vallee	James	Arthur	1909	1975
Vallee	Elizabeth	Frances Rogers	1908	4/7/2002
Vance	John	E.	1906	1965
Vance	Mabel		1906	1980
Vickers-Smith	John		03/28/50	12/9/1924
Vickers-Smith	Ormond		03/09/96	4/28/1975
Vickers-Smith	Gladys	L.	1910	1991
Vickers-Smith	Natalie	Vivian	03/19/24	2/12/1977
Vickers-Smith	Frank		1894	1895
Wall	David	T.	1869	1941

LAST NAME	FIRST NAME	MIDDLE NAME/S	BIRTH	DEATH
Wall	Mary	Elizabeth	1876	1962
Wall	David	Leslie	1901	1974
Wall	Leita	Wallings	1907	1988
Wall	Nathan	L.	03/02/15	9/7/2006
Washburn	Lillian	Fiske	1895	1978
Watson	Florence	E.	1894	1995
Wellhoner	Sarah	Lytle	11/08/17	8/22/1983
West	Annie		1866	1932
West	Cornelius		1865	1951
West	Wilbur	Ernest	8/29/1895	11/11/1966
Wheelock	Marjorie	R.	06/21/36	07/06/98
White	Myrtle	Caroline	11/01/10	07/01/02
White	Myrtle	Caroline	01/21/62	01/21/62
White	Allan	H.	08/05/35	?/?/1969
White	Theodore	L. Sr.	1901	12/24/1986
White	Myrtle	Kay	11/01/10	2/1/1982
Whitney	Bruce	Kendall	1899	1991
Wightman	Nellie	Goodridge	05/23/62	4/30/1950
Wightman	Elisha	Dabell	1863	1931
Wightman	Carrie	Goodridge	1/3/1869	1/19/1958
Williams	Alfred		1917	1995
Williams	Doris		1921	1989
Williamson	Unknown		NIL	NIL
Windhorst	Fred	William	7/12/1893	12/26/1997
Windhorst	Florence	Peacock	1/18/1893	9/8/1979
Whitney	Bruce	Kendall	1899	1991
Woodbridge	Dr. Mary	Newell	1871	?/?/1964

Active Members of Record
December 31, 2009

June Akerlund
Terry and Sheri Banks
Richard and Charlotte Barringer
Parker and Charlotte Bauer
Katie Bauer
Stephanie Bauer
Valerie Bauer
Ted and Judy Bedell
Donna Bott
Darrell Braden
Patricia Braden
Madge Brown
Susy Brown
John and Shirley Buzzell
Clifford and Helga Cail
James and Jane Campbell
Pat Casson
Russell and Dianne Casson
Henry and Mary Childs
Terry Colla
Mary Beth Cunningham
Janet Dearcopp
Andy and Christine Dommerich
Diane Donovan
Greta Fadden
Robert and Annette Freeman
Robert and Joanne Gearhardt
Vicki Gordon
Lillian Hammond
Joan Hardesty

Betty Hastings
Dorothy Heckters
Sara Herman
Eleanor Howarth
Jean Howe
Hugh and Ruth Hughston
Patricia Isaacson
Brad and Mary Ann Jameson
Rod and Kathy Jones
Ty Justison
Wayne and Frances Justison
Walt Karwasinski
Pauline Kepner
Don Kirby
Waldemar and Virginia Krzywicki
Shelly Leon
Robert and Marilyn Limberg
Peg Lipniskas
Neven and Ann-Marie Matthews
Lucillle Michaels
Rob Michaels
Sandy Murray
John and Mary Jo Neidow
Robert and Elaine Pearson
Beverly Pignetti
Jean Pratt
Donald and Barbara Pruitt
Sharon Redding
Joseph and Carol Regna
Elwynn and Patricia Roth
Amy Rowell
Gary Sarto
George Schemanske
Jeanette Schotta
Phillip and Kay Shannon

Lee and Charlotte Shawcross
Shelly Sikes
Judy Sipperley
Gary and Julie Sligh
Carter Sligh
Graham Sligh
Mary Sligh
Frank Smith
Joseph and Elaine Smith
Frances Spedding
John and Candy Storey
Patti Taylor
Harold and PatriciaTopping
Ray and Janet Trudeau
Carol Turner
Norman Turner
John and Patsy Tyler
Jerold and Carol Wang

Associate Priests

Sara Dover
E. Michael Rowell
Marnie Silk-Wright
Joan Watson

List of Sources

NOTE: Copies of, and findings from, much of the research done for this book have been organized and boxed and are available to serious researchers upon request to the Holy Trinity church office.

Books

Bott, D.R.S. *The Chetwynd Chronicles*. Crowder Publishing, 2013.

Elliott, E.J. *Elliott's Florida Encyclopedia*. Jacksonville, FL, 1889.

Gouveia, William F. *Pioneer Trails of Lake County*. W.F. Gouveia, 1989.

Hayes, Edward, and Weber, Betty Ann. *The Florida One-Day Trip Book: 52 Offbeat Excursions In and Around Orlando*. 1st ed. EPM, 1981.

Kennedy, William Thomas. *History of Lake County, Florida*. St. Augustine, FL, Record Co., 1929.

Kimmons-Johnson, Karen, comp. *The Story of Lady Lake*. Lady Lake (FL) Historical Society, 2011.

Paddock, Dorothy Goodnoh, comp. *In the Beauty of Holiness; a History of Holy Trinity Episcopal Church, Fruitland Park, Florida*. Leesburg, FL, Ford Press, 1976.

Vickers-Smith, Lillian D. *The History of Fruitland Park*. Fruitland Park (FL) Chamber of Commerce, 1924.

Magazine and newspaper articles

Bosanquet, Elaine and Richard. "Fair Oaks." Document at Leesburg (FL) Heritage Society.. No citation information.

Campbell, Ramsey. "When Orange Industry Turned Blue." *Orlando Sentinel* 04 Feb. 1995.

"Fruit." *Suniland*. 1925.

Hendricks, Norma. "Dalmation didn't let anyone stand in his way." *The Commercial*, Leesburg, FL 11 June 1979.

Hendricks, Norma. "Fair Oaks built by English bachelor." *The Commercial*, Leesburg, FL. Undated.

King, Lee. "Lake's Landed Gentry. *Orlando Sentinel*, 15 Oct. 2000.

Pinsky, Mark I. "Church Leader Avoids Dispute." *Orlando Sentinel* 23 Dec. 1997.

Pinsky, Mark I. "Episcopal Diocese Rejects Gay Stand." *Orlando Sentinel* 21 Sept. 2003.

Powers, Ormund. "In Early Days, Vickers-Smith Blazed a New Trail for Women in Journalism. *Orlando Sentinel*, 15 May 1996.

Powers, Ormund. "Slick Salesmen Helped Cities Grow at Turn of Century." *Orlando Sentinel*, 30 June 1999.

Reed, Rick. "Reminisce" column about Bertha Hereford Hall. *Daily Commercial*, Leesburg, FL. Undated.

Reed, Rick. "Reminisce" column about R.F.E. Cooke's death. *Daily Commercial,* Leesburg, FL. Undated.

Reed, Rick. "Reminisce" column about the British invasion of Fruitland Park in the 1880s. *Daily Commercial,* Leesburg, FL. Undated.

Reed, Rick. "Reminisce" column, "Adams visits winter home of Annie Oakley." *Daily Commercial,* Leesburg, FL 23 March 2012.

Reed, Rick. "Reminisce" column, "Longtime Leesburg mayor key figure in grape industry." *Daily Commercial,* Leesburg, FL, 27 Sept. 2009.

"The Rev. Margaret Ingalls, rector, inherited preaching genes." *Central Florida Episcopalian* Orlando, FL Mid.-Sept. 1993.

Miscellaneous

The American Church Almanac and Year Book Protestant Episcopal Almanac and Parochial List 1893-1916, The Episcopal Church.

Archival material. Lake County Historical Society, Tavares, FL.

Archival material. Leesburg (FL) Heritage Society.

Archival material. St. James Episcopal Church, Leesburg, FL.

Bott, Donna. "Sealed in Sewickley?" Research results. 2008.

"A Brief History of the Episcopal Church in Florida." 2004.

Davis, The Rev. Ernest. "A Self-Guided Tour of Holy Trinity Episcopal Church, Fruitland Park, Florida." Undated.

Davis, The Rev. Ernest. "Holy Trinity Episcopal Church, Fruitland Park, Florida – Church Tour Data." 1991.

Documents involving St. John's Protestant Episcopal Church , Montclair, FL. Lake County Historical Society, Leesburg, FL.

"Fruitland Park." Phase I CRAS of the Gardenia Trail Phase II Project. Southeastern Archaeological Research. 2008.

Great Freeze at Fair Oaks information on microfilm. John C. Hitt Library, University of Central Florida, Orlando.

Heritage Faith Challenge, Fruitland Park's Centennial (booklet). Fruitland Park, FL, 1976.

Jones, Rod. "Multi-Site Presentation to Congregation 1/12/03." Holy Trinity Episcopal Church, Fruitland Park, FL.

McCullough, Mabel Millard, and Millard, Annie. Letter to St. John's Episcopal Church, Montclair. Lake County Historical Society, Leesburg, FL. Undated.

Missionary Jurisdiction of Southern Florida Journals, 1892-1915.

Newell, Nancy Ayers. "A History of Holy Trinity Episcopal Church, Fruitland Park, Florida." Undated.

Schofield, Maria J., comp. *The City of Fruitland Park, Florida, Today 2001* (booklet).

Sligh, Julie. Testimonial posted on church hotline, Oct. 2, 2010, about Holy Trinity Episcopal School. Holy Trinity Episcopal Church, Fruitland Park, FL.

"Testimonial Dinner Honoring Reverend Frederick N. Paddock and Mrs. Dorothy Paddock." Holy Trinity Episcopal Church. 19 June 1981.

Websites and web pages

"Biography of William R. Newell." *Christian Classics Ethereal Library*. 19 April 2012. <http://www.ccel.org/ccel/newell>

"Bishop John Howe, Diocese of Central Florida, on the Anglican Covenant." *Stand Firm*. 20 Dec. 2009. <http://www.standfirminfaith.com/?/sf/page/25164>

"Black History: St. Cyprian's Historic Episcopal Church, by Amy Howard; Episcopal Church in Florida." *Augustine.com* 24 June 2010. <http://www.augustine.com/history/black_history/st_cyprians/index.php>

"Blackford Family Papers, 1742-1953." Collection No. 01912. Louis Round Wilson Special Collections Library, University of North Carolina, Chapel Hill. <http://www.lib.unc.edu/mss/inv/b/Blackford_Family.html>

"A Brief History of the Diocese." The Episcopal Diocese of Central Florida, Orlando. c2010. <http://www.cfdiocese.org/about/brief-history-diocese>

"The Diocese of Florida; a Brief History." The Episcopal Diocese of Florida, Jacksonville. <http://www.diocesefl.org/about-us/the-diocese/history-of-the-diocese-of-Florida.aspx>

"History of Our Church." *Corpus Christi Episcopal Church,* Okahumpka, FL 28 Oct. 2011. <http://corpuschristiepiscopal.org>

"The History of St. George." *St. George Episcopal Church,* The Villages, FL 28 Oct. 2011. <http://www.stgeorge-episcopal.net>

"A History of the Episcopal Diocese of Southeast Florida." The Episcopal Diocese of Southeast Florida, Miami. 24 June 2010. <http://www.diosef.org/about-us/diocesan-history/index.shtml

"Holyoke Transcript-Telegram." *Wikipedia,* 14 Sept. 2010. <http://en.wikipedia.org/wiki/Holyoke_Transcript-Telegram>

"Leesburg, Florida – History." *Wikipedia.* <http://en.wikipedia.org/wiki/Leesburg,_Florida>

"McKay Scholarship Program." Florida Department of Education, Office of Independent Education & Parental Choice, Tallahassee, FL 27 Sept. 2011. <http://www.floridaschoolchoice.org/information/mckay/

Nunley, Jan. "Fall special conventions, meetings ponder church's direction." *Episcopal News Service Archive. 25 Sept. 2003.* <http://www.ecusa.anglican.org/3577_19494_ENG_HTM.htm>

Rajtar, Steve. "Fruitland Park Historical Trail." c2008. <http://reocities.com/Yosemite/Rapids/8428/hikeplans/fruitland_park/planfruitland.html>

Untitled. St. James Episcopal Church, Leesburg, FL. 26 Jan. 2010. <http://www.stjames-leesburg.org/index.php?page=History>

"What is a FAITH ALIVE Weekend?" *Faith Alive,* Albuquerque, NM, c2008. <http://www.faithalive.org/>

"What is Carpenter Gothic Architecture?" 5 March 2010. <http://www.wisegeek.com/what-is-carpenter-gothic-architecture.htm>

"What is the National Episcopal Cursillo?" *National Episcopal Cursillo,* Conway, SC 07 July 2011. <http://www.nationalepiscopalcursillo.org/>

Interviews, etc.

Bauer, Katie. Telephone interview. 2011.

Bauer, Parker and Charlotte. Personal interview. 2011.

Bauer, Stephanie and Valerie. Personal interview. 2011.

Brown, Suzy. Personal interview. 2011.

Buzzell, John and Shirley. Personal interview and written information. 2011.

Casson, Russell and Dianne. Personal interview and written information. 2010-11.

Davis, The Rev. Ernest. Telephone interview and written material. 2011.

Hastings, Betty., and Justison, Frances. Personal interview. 2011.

Ingalls, The Rev. Margaret. Telephone interview. 2011.

Krzywicki, Wally and Ginny. Personal interview. 2011.

Paddock, Dorothy. Telephone interview. 2012.

Peterman, Helen. Telephone interview. 2011.

Redding, Sharon. Personal interview and emailed information. 2011.

Sutherland, Deacon Richard. Personal interview. 2011.

Tyler, John. Personal interview. 2012.

Walters, The Rev. William. Telephone interview. 2011.

Holy Trinity records and files

Churchyard records

Guild minutes

Guild scrapbook, 1950's and 1960's

Historical documents (including Bucket and Dipper Club minutes on microfilm)

May Festival and Autumn Extravaganza fliers

Parish register

Service bulletins

Service register

(Trinity) Tidings

Vestry minutes

About the author

IVAN FORD is a snowbird who lives the majority of the year in the Traverse City area in northwestern Lower Michigan. He was a public secondary school librarian for most of his 35-year career in education and a journalism instructor and school publications adviser for about two-thirds of it. Retiring in 2004, he started spending winters in Lady Lake, and regularly attending Holy Trinity, early the following year.

He said that the idea of his writing an updated history of this church came about at a "get acquainted" lunch he had with Fr. Michael Rowell and in a subsequent conversation with Donna Bott. When these two learned of his teaching background, his interests in American history of all sorts, and his willingness to devote time to doing something for the church, they suggested this project.

Ford is single.

Coming Home is his first book.